CONVERSATIONS WITH THE MOST HIGH

Other New Hope books by
Jennifer Kennedy Dean

Live a Praying Life®: Open Your Life to God's Power and Provision

Live a Praying Life: Open Your Life to God's Power and Provision
Bible Study—Tenth Anniversary Edition

Live a Praying Life: Open Your Life to God's Power and Provision
DVD Leader Kit—Tenth Anniversary Edition

Live a Praying Life: A Daily Look at God's Power and Provision
Journal

Clothed with Power: A Six-Week Journey to Freedom, Power, and Peace

Clothed with Power DVD

Altar'd: Experience the Power of Resurrection

Life Unhindered! Five Keys to Walking in Freedom

Secrets Jesus Shared: Kingdom Insights Revealed Through the Parables

Secrets Jesus Shared: Kingdom Insights Revealed Through the Parables
DVD Leader Kit

The Power of Small: Think Small to Live Large

Pursuing the Christ: Prayers for Christmastime

Heart's Cry: Principles of Prayer

CONVERSATIONS WITH THE MOST HIGH: 365 DAYS IN GOD'S PRESENCE

Jennifer Kennedy Dean

NEW HOPE
PUBLISHERS
Gospel-Centered. Missions-Driven.

BIRMINGHAM, ALABAMA

New Hope® Publishers
PO Box 12065
Birmingham, AL 35202-2065
NewHopeDigital.com
New Hope Publishers is a division of WMU®.

Library of Congress Control Number: 2014947068

ISBN-10: 1-59669-393-2
ISBN-13: 978-1-59669-393-7
N144102 • 1114 • 4M1

Dedication

To my mom
Audrey Kennedy, who has lived her life in conversation
with the Most High.

Introduction

This is an expansion of a book I wrote some years ago, 1996 to be exact, originally titled *Secret Place of the Most High*. It grows out of my lifelong pursuit to hear the Eternal Word speak His eternal words in my present moment. I love to know that the words of Scripture are the vehicles through which He hand delivers His personal message into my heart. That they go far beyond imparting information; they produce transformation.

I do not claim to be taking dictation from God, or hearing what others do not. Instead, this is the way God reveals Himself to me. The words of Scripture sit and ferment in my heart and come back to me in silent moments, spoken in words that touch me in a present and personal way.

When I was just a kid, I came across Psalm 91:1 in the King James Version: "He that dwelleth in the secret place of the most High shall abide under the shadow of the Almighty." It completely captivated me. The words spoke to my introverted, hermit personality. I love secret places. Somehow those words just clung to my heart and whispered to me of an intimacy I could have with the Most High.

Over the years I ran across certain authors and thinkers who seemed to have that same wonder for the invitation to the secret place. Thomas Kelley first introduced me to the idea that I could live in a state of prayer, and from that idea came the phrase that has defined my ministry for over 40 years: *Live a Praying Life*®. Over the years, others in that vein influenced me to believe that God would speak to me from His Word in specific and personal ways. He would take His words recorded in Scripture and speak them right into the depths of my heart.

I expanded the original text to 365 days. I started this years ago and kept on expanding. I pray that the Holy Spirit will speak His detailed and specific words to your heart.

January

JANUARY 1
Child,

Walk in newness. I have called you to journey with Me into new territories and new directions. I have not invited you into rote attendance, or stale repetition. Every step you take is into new terrains. You must keep your eyes on Me because I am the Way. The kind of newness I've called you to keeps getting newer. It is the opposite of the material world. Nothing new stays new in the earth's environment, but in My eternal kingdom, new gets newer. Shake off the old, the staid, the worn-out, and walk in newness.

"Therefore we have been buried with Him through baptism into death, so that as Christ was raised from the dead through the glory of the Father, so we too might walk in newness of life" (ROMANS 6:4 NASB).

JANUARY 2
Father,

I am at home in You and You are at home in me. A perfect fit. No other relationship, no other possession, no other accomplishment . . . nothing is as cozy and just right as Your presence. Teach me to live always aware of and alive to You in me.

"They feast on the abundance of your house; you give them drink from your river of delights" (PSALM 36:8).

JANUARY 3

Child,

You can stay quiet in My presence. You don't have to entertain or impress Me. You don't need to win Me over. I'm yours. I'm all yours. I'm forever yours. Let that be enough between us now.

"I am my beloved's, and my beloved is mine . . . I am my beloved's, and his desire is for me" (SONG OF SONGS 6:3; 7:10 KJV).

JANUARY 4

Child,

My presence is not wispy or insubstantial. I have come to reside in you through My Spirit. I have taken up residence. I'm not just visiting. You don't have to fret and put on airs. My presence anchors your life and gives you a center of gravity. Just be. You'll find that *I am.*

"Salt, when dissolved in water, may disappear, but it does not cease to exist. We can be sure of its presence by tasting the water. Likewise, the indwelling Christ, though unseen, will be made evident to others from the love which he imparts to us."

—SADHU SUNDAR SINGH

JANUARY 5

Child,

My presence in you transforms you. My presence in you is active and powerful and irrepressible and unrestrained. I never stop working. I never sleep or take a break. Even while you sleep, I work. While you rest, I accomplish. I do in you what you cannot do in yourself. Then I do through you what you on your own could not.

"For myself I feel that the Lord must do the whole work of restoration for me, for I am powerless to do anything for myself. He must give me the desire even to be restored. I have been asking Him to do this, and I trust not in vain. Then He must also help me to view properly the earthly things for which I long, so that I will not grieve over their loss. And He must so satisfy me with Himself that all other joys will seem weak and poor in comparison."

—HANNAH WHITALL SMITH, *The Christian's Secret of a Holy Life: the unpublished writings of Hannah Whitall Smith*

JANUARY 6

Father,

Remind me that the joy You offer in Your presence is so much more than the fleeting surges of happiness that rise and fall, come and go, when I look outside You for satisfaction. I was created by You and for You, and nothing temporal satisfies. When I have worn myself out trying to arrange my outward circumstances to fit my idea of happiness—when I'm broken and defeated—there You are. The very joy I've been chasing waits for me in Your unchanging presence.

"Is the peace of God in the soul disturbed by things down here? No, never! If waters break in stormy currents against a rock, the rock is unmoved; it is only the waters that are disturbed."

—G. V. WIGRAM

JANUARY 7
Child,

The purpose for My presence in You is to show Myself through You. I change you, and cleanse you, and work in you so that you will be a transparent vessel through which I display Myself. So that the image you project of Me is accurate. You can be sure that My love for you is, as gently as possible, working out your highest purpose.

"The whole activity of the Lord Jesus on earth as Man was the Father's activity in the Son, through the eternal Spirit, as Jesus presented His body to the Father through the Spirit. This is true also for us. Our spirituality is simply our availability to God for His divine activity, and the form of this activity is irrelevant."

—MAJOR W. IAN THOMAS, *The Indwelling Life of Christ*

JANUARY 8
Child,

Sometimes when you seek Me, it seems that I am nowhere to be found. That when you look for Me, you see only nothingness. You experience Me as an absence rather than a presence. You feel desolate and alone. My child, My presence is not a feeling, but a reality. Count on it. Know Me to be present. Emotions come and go, but I remain. "And surely I am with you always, to the very end of the age" (Matthew 28:20).

"Faith has nothing to do with feelings or with impressions, with improbabilities or with outward experiences. If we desire to couple such things with faith, then we are no longer resting on the Word of God, because faith needs nothing of the kind. Faith rests on the naked Word of God. When we take Him at His Word, the heart is at peace."

—GEORGE MÜELLER

JANUARY 9

Is there anything in your life or experience that I do not have the power to handle? To do so perfectly and willingly and lovingly? Then rest. I have not left you to work things out the best you can. I have given you My presence. My person. I take full responsibility for you and everything in your life. Just yield.

"Cast your cares on the LORD and he will sustain you; he will never let the righteous be shaken" (PSALM 55:22).

JANUARY 10
Child,

How many ways have I described My presence? In you, with you, on you, for you, through you. My presence saturates your life. Floods your being. All of Me in all of you. Take the knowledge of My presence with you in everything you do, everything you encounter, every word you speak, every thought you think. Imagine how it will change the contours of your day to be present to My presence.

"Paul acknowledges that, though his flesh or old man died with Christ, he is still living a life in his body. He chooses every minute to live that life with the confidence that the Lord Jesus is able to express Himself through the body and personality of Paul. He chooses to live out his life in an altar'd state, with his flesh surrendered to its crucifixion and his spirit alive to the presence of Jesus. Present to the Presence."

—JENNIFER KENNEDY DEAN, *Altar'd*

JANUARY 11
Father,

To think that I was created and fitted to be inhabited by You is beyond the scope of my finite mind. Until I became Your dwelling place, I could only yearn. Meaning, purpose, fulfillment—all elusive dreams, shimmering goals that lacked substance or definition. Then You. Your presence in me fills my emptiness and causes my desert places to flow with springs of living water.

"In the 'secret of God's tabernacle' no enemy can find us, and no troubles can reach us. The 'pride of man' and the 'strife of tongues' find no entrance into the 'pavilion' of God. The 'secret of his presence' is a more secure refuge than a thousand Gibraltars. I do not mean that no trials come. They may come in abundance, but they cannot penetrate into the sanctuary of the soul, and we may dwell in perfect peace even in the midst of life's fiercest storms."

—Hannah Whitall Smith, *God of All Comfort*

JANUARY 12
Child,

I created you for joy. You can't live without it. You seek it, crave it, pursue it, try to manufacture it. Like your body can't live without water, your spirit can't live without joy. I designed you this way so that you would finally turn to Me as your only joy. My indwelling presence is the only way to joy. Turn away from other things and look only to Me. "All my springs of joy are in you" (Psalm 87:7 NASB).

"Joy marks the life of person whose heart belongs exclusively to Jesus. Joy is impossible to define. It can be known only by experiencing it. Joy

is an emotion that comes out of your spirit. The flesh has a shadow version of joy called happiness or pleasure. But the flesh's version is flat, one-dimensional, and transitory. Unlike happiness, which comes and goes with circumstances, joy is spiritual. Joy is in effect continually because it is based on the solid and unchanging life of Jesus."

—JENNIFER KENNEDY DEAN, *Altar'd*

JANUARY 13

Jesus,

I am taken by wonder at the idea of Your very life flowing through me like a vine's life flows into the branch. No separation. You have closed up the gap between us by Your life flowing in me. Life flows from You right into me. I'm picturing it. Awed by it. And then You tell me: "I have told you this so that my joy may be in you and that your joy may be complete" (John 15:11). You flowing in me is the formula for how I can experience complete joy.

"One of the hallmarks of Jesus' life is joy. Unbridled, unrestrained joy. And flesh can't counterfeit it. . . . The joy that a Spirit-led Christian experiences is the very joy of the indwelling Christ being expressed through his personality. Jesus, in His prayer recorded in John 17, said that everything He was asking from the Father on behalf of His disciples was 'so that they may have the full measure of my joy within them' (John 17:13)."

—JENNIFER KENNEDY DEAN, *Altar'd*

JANUARY 14

Child,

My presence is your peace. Today whatever confronts you, let My peace reign. Am I afraid? Am I surprised? Am I overwhelmed?

Then lean into Me and let My peace be yours. I can make a direct deposit of My peace into your heart when your heart is wide open to Me.

"Even the smell of the aloes, and the myrrh, and the cassia, which drop from his perfumed garments, causes the sick and the faint to grow strong. Let there be but a moment's leaning of the head upon that gracious bosom, and a reception of his divine love into our poor cold hearts, and we are cold no longer, but glow like seraphs, equal to every labor, and capable of every suffering, [sic] If we know that Jesus is with us, every power will be developed, and every grace will be strengthened, and we shall cast ourselves into the Lord's service with heart, and soul, and strength; therefore is the presence of Christ to be desired above all things."

—C. H. SPURGEON, *Morning and Evening: Daily Readings*

JANUARY 15

Father,

There are times when my thoughts seem to be pinging from here to there, bouncing off this idea, then that fear, then another quagmire. Peace eludes me. I can't bring my mind to rest on any one solution. I can't feel as if I've found an answer to my dilemma and I am filled with anxiety and uncertainty. Then I remember that You are present. It's not up to me. And there—in You, not in a solution—I find rest.

"True faith, by a mighty effort of the will, fixes its gaze on our Divine helper, and there finds it possible and wise to lose its fears. It is madness to say, I will not be afraid; it is wisdom and peace to say, I will trust and not be afraid."

—ALEXANDER MACLAREN, *Week-day Evening Addresses,*
Delivered in Manchester

JANUARY 16
Jesus,

Because of Your presence in me and with me, I find the peace that surpasses understanding—a gift from You. Then, to my surprise, I begin to find the understanding that peace produces. When my riotous emotions and turbulent thoughts settle in Your presence, I find a new perspective emerging—a new grid through which to see my situation.

"Blessed are the single-hearted, for they shall enjoy much peace . . . If you refuse to be hurried and pressed, if you stay your soul on God, nothing can keep you from that clearness of spirit which is life and peace. In that stillness you know what His will is."

—Amy Carmichael

JANUARY 17
Child,

Give your attention to My presence and I will carry you out into the deep waters. Cling to Me. I won't throw you into the deep end and let you flail. I'll carry you there.

"'Launch out into the deep' (Luke 5:4). How deep He does not say. The depth into which we launch will depend upon how perfectly we have given up the shore, and the greatness of our need, and the apprehension of our possibilities. The fish were to be found in the deep, not in the shallow water."

—Mrs. Charles E. (L. B. E.) Cowman, *Streams in the Desert Daily Devotional*, February 29

JANUARY 18
Child,

Rest in My presence because of who I am. Do you believe that I am sovereign and powerful? Then know that the circumstances of your life are under My control. Do you believe that I love you completely? Then know that these very circumstances are moving you into My highest plan for you. Let My presence be your peace.

"So long as we are occupied with any other object than God Himself, there will be neither rest for the heart nor peace for the mind. But when we receive all that enters our lives as from His hand, then no matter what may be our circumstances or surroundings—whether in a hovel or prison-dungeon, or at a martyr's stake—we shall be enabled to say, 'The lines are fallen unto me in pleasant places' (Psa. 16:6). But, that is the language of faith, not of sight nor of sense."
—A. W. PINK, *Studies in the Scriptures, volume 5*

JANUARY 19
Child,

As long as My presence is the tower from which you survey the landscape of your life, circumstances will not dictate your emotions. Let My presence be your vantage point.

"What I am urging is simply that you become delightfully detached from the pressure of circumstance, so that it ceases to be the criterion in the decisions you make. You do as you are told, whether God's instructions appear to be compatible with the immediate situation or not, and you leave God to vindicate Himself and to justify the course of action upon which you have embarked at His command. You will

not need to know what He plans to do with you . . . you simply need
to know Him."

—Major W. Ian Thomas, *The Indwelling Life of Christ*

JANUARY 20
Child,

Today, remember that My presence is constant. I will never, ever leave you. I am fully present to you all the time. An undercurrent of prayer flows between us every minute, whether consciously offered or flowing wordlessly. By My presence in you, heaven is always connected to earth.

"The purpose of prayer is to reveal the presence of God equally present, all the time, in every condition."

—Oswald Chambers, *My Utmost for His Highest*

JANUARY 21
Father,

I love Your presence. I love the respite when You and I can sit quietly and I can rest all my cares, all my personality, all my anxieties on You without having to explain or defend. I am not concerned about coming up with the right words to make You understand, because You know better than I know. I can just breathe.

"It is not necessary to maintain a conversation when we are in the presence of God. We can come into His presence and rest our weary souls in quiet contemplation of Him. Our groanings, which cannot be uttered, rise to Him and tell Him better than words how dependent we are upon Him."

—Ole Hallesby, *Prayer*

JANUARY 22
Child,

There is nothing outside of My presence that will delight you. I know because I designed you. What is it that you think is lacking in your life, the possession of which would add some missing joy? Be assured that if any absent possession or relationship or circumstance would produce what you imagine it would produce, I would be sure you had it.

"'I said to the Lord, "You are my Lord; apart from You I have no good thing"' (Psalm 16:2). You don't need to seek any further. You've found Him, you've found everything. There is nothing good apart from Him. Surrender your heart. Altar your life. Give Him such full reign in your life that He can flood you and saturate you with His power and His presence. Nothing outside of Him is worth holding on to."

—Jennifer Kennedy Dean, *Altar'd*

JANUARY 23
Father,

Let me be so settled in Your presence that everything else is defined by it. If I could count the hours spent being anxious about possibilities that never materialized! If I could measure the weight of fearing things or events that turned out to be blips on the radar screen! Teach me to let Your presence be the barometer of my life.

"Forbid, O Lord God, that my thoughts to-day should be wholly occupied with the world's passing show. . . . Grant rather that each day may do something to strengthen my hold upon the unseen world."

—John Baillie, *A Diary of Private Prayer*

JANUARY 24
Child,

Here in My presence, no words are necessary. Here you are safe, and loved, and fully known. I understand things about you that you don't understand about yourself, and love you completely—not *in spite of* those things, but *in* those things. I don't have to overlook anything about you in order to cherish you with all My heart. You are Mine.

I invite you into My secret place, where the reward is far beyond any reward you can earn or recognition you can gain. Time seeking My face is not wasted time, but rather it is time that brings reward. My reward is Myself.

"But when you pray, go into your room, close the door and pray to your Father, who is unseen. Then your Father, who sees what is done in secret, will reward you" (Matthew 6:6).

"Come, and however feeble you feel, just wait in His presence. As a feeble, sickly invalid is brought out into the sunshine to let its warmth go through him, come . . . and sit and wait there with one thought: Here I am, in the sunshine of His love."
—ANDREW MURRAY, "WAITING ON GOD: STRONG AND OF GOOD COURAGE"

JANUARY 25
Father,

The more aware and sensitive I am to Your presence, the more moldable I become. My softened heart becomes clay in Your hands. You can mold and shape my life so that I am an expression of You. More and more, my interaction with others becomes an exposition of You. May it ever increase.

"The abiding characteristic of a spiritual man is the interpretation of the Lord Jesus Christ to himself, and the interpretation to others of the purposes of God. The one concentrated passion of the life is Jesus Christ."

—OSWALD CHAMBERS, *My Utmost for His Highest*

JANUARY 26

Father,

The light of Your countenance acclimates my vision so that I see everyone else in the light of Your presence. It changes the way I perceive others. It softens the harsh angles and bathes them in heavenly hues so that their beauty is readily apparent.

"Above all, keep much in the presence of God. Never see the face of man until you have seen his face, who is our life, our all."

—ROBERT MURRAY McCHEYNE

JANUARY 27

Father,

I realize that You are my dwelling place, not my filling station. Your continual presence is as necessary to me as air to my lungs. I cannot take one right step except in Your power. I cannot think one right thought except under Your guidance. I need You every second that I live. In You I live and move and have my being.

"A man can no more take in a supply of grace for the future than he can eat enough for the next six months or take sufficient air into his lungs at one time to sustain life for a week. We must draw upon God's boundless store of grace from day to day as we need it."

—D. L. MOODY, *Sovereign Grace*

JANUARY 28
Child,

Your makeup requires a continual filling of My Spirit. You don't get filled up, then go out and use up that power, then come back for more. No. You stay connected to My presence and the filling never stops. Like vine and branch, life flows without interruption. My ever-presence is your empowering.

"Christ is not a reservoir but a spring. His life is continual, active and ever passing on with an outflow as necessary as its inflow. If we do not perpetually draw the fresh supply from the living Fountain, we shall either grow stagnant or empty, [sic] It is, therefore, not so much a perpetual fullness as a perpetual filling."

—A. B. SIMPSON

JANUARY 29
Child,

Did you think that My presence was a place of scolding and shaming? Your enemy would love for you to think so. But My presence is the one place where you are loved unconditionally, accepted unreservedly, cherished immeasurably. I can see the you that you are becoming. I'm not blind to your sins and your weaknesses, but I love you in them and through them. I knew about them before I called you. You are no surprise to Me.

"What elevates the human soul and empowers it to live in the fullness of its created purpose is not religious intimidation or new rules or an anxiety induced by spiritual scoldings. It is faith in the promise that the enjoyment sin brings is fleeting and futile, but

at God's right hand, and in the presence of his radiant glory, are pleasures evermore (Psalm 16:11)."

—SAM STORMS

JANUARY 30

Child,

In the spiritual realm, I'm your atmosphere. I'm the air your spirit breathes. I'm not a distant deity for whom you must search. I have come to you. I have wooed you. I have initiated intimacy and relationship with you. Just respond. Just receive.

"Perfect fellowship is attained by His perfect and stainless offering of Himself. All is clear between God and man. For it is 'for us' He enters this presence and fellowship; not that He alone may enjoy it, but that we may enter into the rest and blessedness that He won for us."

—K. S. WUEST, *Wuest's Word Studies from the Greek New Testament: For the English Reader*

JANUARY 31

Jesus,

Transfixed by Your beauty, enthralled by Your love for me. One glance and I am lost to all but You. The reality of You dawns on me, and everything else loses its allure. What can compare to the glory of You? Once seeing You, the wonder of Your poured-out love eclipses all else. Anything other than You now looks worn out and dingy. You are my everything.

"And a blessed truth it is, for where Jesus is, love becomes inflamed. Of all the things in the world that can set the heart burning, there is nothing like the presence of Jesus!"

—C. H. SPURGEON, *Morning and Evening: Daily Readings*

February

FEBRUARY 1
Child,

Look to Me. Lock your gaze onto My face. Don't try to navigate by guessing or by your own sonar. Move in step with Me. Stay in tandem with Me. With your eyes fixed on Me, you will not wander. You will walk with certainty through any landscape.

"In all the travels of the Israelites, whenever the cloud lifted from above the tabernacle, they would set out; but if the cloud did not lift, they did not set out—until the day it lifted. So the cloud of the LORD was over the tabernacle by day, and fire was in the cloud by night, in the sight of all the Israelites during all their travels" (EXODUS 40:36–38).

FEBRUARY 2
Child,

The light of My countenance is always with you. I never, never, never leave you, abandon you, forsake you, or forget you. You are My highest priority and the focus of My thoughts and the target of My love. As if you were My one and only concern, My heart is filled with you. Always. Live this day in full awareness of Me.

"This day is Your gift to me; I take it, Lord, from Your hand, and thank You for the wonder of it. God, be with me in this Your day, every day and every way . . . All that I am, Lord, I place into Your hands. All that I do, Lord, I place into Your hands. Everything I work for I place into Your hands. Everything I hope for I place into Your hands. The troubles that weary me I place into Your hands. The thoughts that disturb me I place into Your hands. I place into Your hands, Lord, the choices that I face. . . . May I feel Your presence at the heart of my desire, and so know it for Your desire for me. . . . Help me to find my happiness in my acceptance of what is Your purpose for me: In friendly eyes, in work well done, in quietness born of trust. And, most of all, in the awareness of Your presence in my spirit. Amen."
—OSWALD OF NORTHUMBRIA, CELTIC MONK, AD 605–642

FEBRUARY 3
Child,

Look to Me, and you will find yourself. Look to Me, and you will discover who you were created to be. You will find the life designed just with you in mind. You will begin to live a life that fits, rather than a life that chafes. I am fully invested in bringing you to the apex of your destiny.

"There is still One whose faith in you has never wavered. And how wonderful it is that that one should be Jesus Christ! It was a wonderful dream God dreamed, Christ says, when He created you; it was a stately being that was in His mind when you were fashioned; and I can make you all He meant that you should be."

—A. J. Gossip

FEBRUARY 4
Child,

You look more like Me every day. As you fix your eyes on Me, you are being changed incrementally into My likeness. You mirror My expressions. You see as I see. You talk like Me and walk like Me. I live and love in your world through your life. Keep looking at Me.

"The man who gazes upon and contemplates day by day the face of the Lord Jesus Christ, and who has caught the glow of the reality that the Lord is not a theory but an indwelling power and force in his life, is as a mirror reflecting the glory of the Lord."

—Alan Redpath

FEBRUARY 5

Father,

When I keep my heart and mind stayed on You, it frees me from the tyranny of my self-serving tendencies. I can't look at You and, at the same time, make myself an idol. Created to worship You, I break down under the burden of idolizing myself. But when my heart's eyes are drawn to Your dear face, everything aligns properly and I can trust You with my needs while I worship and adore the One for whom my heart was made.

"The labor of self-love is a heavy one indeed. Think for yourself whether much of your sorrow has not arisen from someone speaking slightingly of you. As long as you set yourself up as a little god to which you must be loyal there will be those who will delight to offer affront to your idol. How then can you hope to have inward peace?"

—A. W. Tozer, *The Pursuit of God*

FEBRUARY 6

Father,

Let my heart be fully Yours. Alert me when a piece of my heart wanders off to the siren-song of the world's empty charms. Call me back to You. Gather up the pieces of my divided heart and reassemble it, affixed to You. I want You to be all I desire. Make it so.

"My dear Jesus, my Savior, is so deeply written in my heart, that I feel confident, that if my heart were to be cut open and chopped to pieces, the name of Jesus would be found written on every piece."

—Ignatius of Antioch

FEBRUARY 7
Jesus,

Riveted by Your much-adored face, I now find beauty in places where before I saw only ugliness. I see hope where I once saw despair; potential instead of failure. Everything looks different because You are my reference point.

"Fix your eyes on Jesus. Lock your gaze on Him. Everything else can be perceived correctly if His presence is the reference point.

Your mind always needs a reference point to correctly see reality. For example, imagine that you see a photograph of an object and the object fills the frame. It looks big. Then you see a photograph of that same object, but held in a person's hand. Now, with the hand as a reference point, your perception of the object's size changes."
—JENNIFER KENNEDY DEAN, *Life Unhindered!*

FEBRUARY 8
Child,

Look into My face until you are sun-blinded by My presence. Until My face is superimposed over every other face you see. Until you see others only through Me. They look different now. Love changes everything.

"It is a good rule never to look into the face of a man in the morning till you have looked into the face of God."
—C. H. SPURGEON, *The Metropolitan Tabernacle Pulpit*

FEBRUARY 9

Father,

Your face is all I seek. Where once I sought to find faith, and love, and holiness in myself so I could bring something to You, now I look away from myself and look only to You. I am devoid of anything that I might offer You for Your service. I bring You my nothing, and in exchange, receive Your everything.

"Do not try to stir and arouse faith from within. . . . You cannot stir up faith from the depths of your heart. Leave your heart, and look into the face of Christ."

—Andrew Murray, *Absolute Surrender and Other Addresses*

FEBRUARY 10

Jesus,

To rest in Your presence and seek Your face accomplishes more in my life than any straining and trying and working to be holy ever has. I think You infect me with Your own holiness and then it is diffused from my heart into my thoughts and activities and responses. I find holiness spreading, surprising me as it turns up where unrighteousness used to be.

"Give up the struggle and the fight; relax in the omnipotence of the Lord Jesus; look up into His lovely face and as you behold Him, He will transform you into His likeness. You do the beholding—He does the transforming. There is no short-cut to holiness."

—Alan Redpath

FEBRUARY 11

Father,

Attune my heart to Your voice. Align my desires with Yours.

Calibrate my steps to the rhythm of Your Spirit. I offer You my whole personality, my every moment, my plans and dreams. Bring all into perfect harmony with Your life in me.

"Every character has an inward spring, let Christ be it. Every action has a key-note, let Christ set it."

—HENRY DRUMMOND, *The Changed Life*

FEBRUARY 12
Child,

In My kingdom, there is no such thing as a small obedience. I never call you to an act or response of obedience that has no purpose, or for which the purpose is other than eternal. On your side of the continuum, it may seem small. It may seem unimportant. But if I call you to it, then it matters. Today, purpose that not one whispered command of Mine will go unnoticed. Put all your senses on alert for My still, small voice, and obey with abandon. Be radical in your obedience today. And trust that it matters.

"My personal life may be crowded with small, petty happenings, altogether insignificant. But if I obey Jesus Christ in the seemingly random circumstances of life, they become pinholes through which I see the face of God. Then, when I stand face to face with God, I will discover that through my obedience thousands were blessed. When God's redemption brings a human soul to the point of obedience, it always produces. If I obey Jesus Christ, the redemption of God will flow through me to the lives of others, because behind the deed of obedience is the reality of Almighty God."

—OSWALD CHAMBERS, *My Utmost for His Highest*

FEBRUARY 13

Child,

Are you grieving things you've lost? Or pining for things longed for, but never possessed? In your most honest, naked moments, do you feel that I have favored others but not you? You can tell Me all about it without fear of disapproval. I know. I read your heart instead of your lips. I see it all. Hear My heart in this: if that for which you yearn would indeed give you what you believe it would, I would have granted it to you. I never withhold good. If you knew as I know, you would make the same decisions I make. You must learn to trust My love for you. Today, begin to trust My wisdom more than you trust your own desires.

"Trust in the LORD with all your heart and lean not on your own understanding; in all your ways submit to him, and he will make your paths straight" (PROVERBS 3:5–6).

FEBRUARY 14

Child,

I am not counting on your strength. I am exploiting your weakness. My strength shows up beautifully where you are weak. You have nothing to prove to Me. I am willing to prove Myself to you. I am willing to guarantee My strength for your weakness. Are you feeling weak in the face of what life has brought you? Are you feeling inadequate to face what lies in front of you? Then you are perfectly positioned for Me to show Myself strong on your behalf. Don't view your weakness as something to be despised, but rather as something to be embraced. Think of your weakness as the well-lit landing strip for My great power.

"But he said to me, 'My grace is sufficient for you, for my power is made perfect in weakness.' Therefore I will boast all the more gladly about my weaknesses, so that Christ's power may rest on me.

That is why, for Christ's sake, I delight in weaknesses, in insults, in hardships, in persecutions, in difficulties. For when I am weak, then I am strong" (2 CORINTHIANS 12:9–10).

FEBRUARY 15
Father,

I surrender all my worry and anxiety to You. Some days, anxious thoughts float around me like a cloud of insects that I might futilely try to bat away. They buzz and swarm. They dive at me, and then flit away before I can get hold of them. I can't even name the free-floating angst that sometimes seems to shroud me and accompany me wherever I go. But I do know You, Almighty, in-control God. I can get hold of You because You have taken hold of me. I refuse to be overwhelmed with little fears when I know the One who cares so much for me that You number the very hairs of my head. Today, I trust Your love for me.

"When my anxious thoughts multiply within me, Your consolations delight my soul" (PSALM 94:19 NASB).

FEBRUARY 16
Child,

Do not fear. How many times do I introduce My message with these words? I know that what confronts your senses seems fearful—I know that your situation looks frightening. That's why I remind you not to follow your perceptions but rather to see My truth. My presence, My power, My might—these are your reality. What is frightening you today? Do you see Me in the midst? I am here now. Your now is in My plan. And I know what I'm doing. Do not fear.

"The beginning of anxiety is the end of faith, and the beginning of true faith is the end of anxiety."

—GEORGE MÜELLER

FEBRUARY 17

Child,

Obey. You know what I am calling you to do. You have been resisting because it puts your pride at risk. You can't control or predict the outcome, so it leaves you feeling exposed and vulnerable. Your resistance means that you are putting yourself in My place. You are overriding My command with your own ideas. Your obedience will open the way for My power to work in its fullness. I love you and will never call you to harm, only to what will benefit you and further My wonderful plan for you. Will you trust Me in this?

"Whoever obeys his command will come to no harm, and the wise heart will know the proper time and procedure" (ECCLESIASTES 8:5).

FEBRUARY 18

Father,

My fears feel true. Your promise can sound far-fetched and unbelievable, while my fears sound reasonable and built on evidence. I'm used to my fears. I've always felt at home in them. But You pursue me and whisper Your love and repeat Your assurances, and Your voice is sweet to my heart's ears. Your words come to life in me. They overpower fear and drown out anxiety. I choose to believe You. I choose to rest my life on Your faithfulness. Help my unbelief.

"Fear is born of Satan, and if we would only take time to think a moment we would see that everything Satan says is founded upon a falsehood. He is the father of lies."

—A. B. Simpson, *Days of Heaven Upon Earth: A Year Book of Scripture Texts and Living Truths*

FEBRUARY 19
Child,

Don't be surprised that life has pain in it. Earth and time are not your home. You are a stranger and alien here. Your home is eternity. So, don't be surprised that earth's landscape is often unfriendly. You were made for another biosphere, and you will never be fully assimilated to your earthly environment. The traversing of this terrain will always include tears and sorrow along the way. I never promised that you will not walk through the Valley of Weeping, but rather that, for you, the Valley of Weeping will be transformed into a place of refreshing springs. My presence makes the wasteland a garden. As you walk through this particular sorrow and heartache, let Me enrich you through it.

"Transiency is stamped on all our possessions, occupations, and delights. We have the hunger for eternity in our souls, the thought of eternity in our hearts, the destination for eternity written on our inmost being, and the need to ally ourselves with eternity proclaimed by the most short-lived trifles of time. Either these things will be the blessing or the curse of our lives. Which do you mean that they shall be for you?"

—Alexander Maclaren, *Sermons Preached in Union Chapel, Manchester*

FEBRUARY 20
Child,

Think about what I have done for you—what I have given you. You are filled with, flooded with, saturated with Jesus. He is Living Water flowing through you. He is the entire Treasure of heaven. He is the Beginning and the End; the Wisdom of the Ages; the repository of eternity's riches—in you. Stop and delight in this. Take it with you when you step into your responsibilities and challenges and opportunities. Cling to this as your reality.

"The Son of God has been poured into us, and we have received him and appropriated him. What a heart-full Jesus must be, for heaven itself cannot contain him!"
　　　　　　　—CHARLES SPURGEON, *Morning and Evening: Daily Readings*

FEBRUARY 21
Child,

Remember that most of My work is invisible to your naked eye. When you look around you and analyze the empirical data of your situation, don't stop there. What you can see does not tell the whole story. My kingdom works underground and beyond sight. What I'm doing cannot be analyzed and measured. I don't give you a daily rundown of My activity. I just call you to trust, to know what you cannot see.

"So we fix our eyes not on what is seen, but on what is unseen, since what is seen is temporary, but what is unseen is eternal" (2 CORINTHIANS 4:18).

FEBRUARY 22
Child,

I created you to be a channel, not a reservoir. I fill you so I can flow from you. It does not comport with your design when you hoard. You miss out on the joy that giving generates. You don't experience the adventure that your life can become. Don't try to play it safe. Don't bury the gifts I have given you. Don't try to hold tight to what you have so you won't find yourself bereft. You are made in My image and I am a Filler Up, a Pourer Out. I will pour in as you pour out. When you give of yourself, or of your resources, or of your gifts—you are not emptying yourself. You are making room for greater filling. Go today and be alert for every opportunity to give without reserve. Reckless obedience is what I'm looking for.

"For whoever has will be given more, and they will have an abundance" (MATTHEW 25:29).

FEBRUARY 23
Father,

Forgive me when I feel dissatisfied with how You are arranging my life. Sometimes I'm like a petulant child. As if Your job in my life were to respond to my whims and carry out my best ideas. Teach me to settle in with You and allow You to speak peace and order into my chaotic, churning thoughts. Bring to the surface the lie that is playing the tune my emotions dance to. When the lie steps out of the background and stands under the light, its ugliness is repulsive and it has no draw on my heart. Let me see as You see. Let the beautiful truth take the stage. Remind me that every time I feel disaffected and displeased with the course You have me on, I have embraced a lie. Lead me in the truth and teach me.

"Make me know Your ways, O LORD; Teach me Your paths. Lead me

in Your truth and teach me, For You are the GOD of my salvation; For You I wait all the day" (PSALM 25:4–5 NASB).

FEBRUARY 24
Child,

Gratitude is the game-changer. No matter what. Remember to be thankful when things are going as you want them to go. Don't forget that every gift comes from Me. This will keep you from taking anything for granted and missing the wonder of My attention to every detail. Remember to be thankful when everything seems to be coming apart at the seams. You can be grateful in the midst of pain and disappointment because you know I am working, and you know I am working things toward a good end. Even when you don't see it, you know it. Praise Me for what you know, not what you see. Praise and gratitude will make all the difference. Try it and see.

"Let us thank God heartily as often as we pray, that we have his Spirit in us to teach us to pray. Thanksgiving will draw our hearts out to God and keep us engaged with him; it will take our attention from ourselves and give the Spirit room in our hearts."
—ANDREW MURRAY, *The Prayer Life*

FEBRUARY 25
Father,

Today, I exchange every worrying thought for thanksgiving. If the situations that worry me were indeed my responsibility— if You were looking to me to solve the problems and unravel the messes—then worry would make perfect sense. I'm not up to the job. I haven't a clue about how to resolve things. You are not depending on me for the answers. I'm looking to You for the answers. Thanksgiving and praise make more sense than worry. I acknowledge that all my stressing and worrying does not change anything except my state of mind. When I could be delighting in You and Your care, instead worry loads me down and steals all my joy. Today, I choose joy.

"We would worry less if we praised more. Thanksgiving is the enemy of discontent and dissatisfaction."

—Harry Ironside

FEBRUARY 26
Child,

I am the True Light. The light I created—the light you know in My creation—is a shadow of Me. I am Your Light. Created light is an illustration of the True Light. The True Light existed before created light and will continue to exist long after created light is no longer necessary. When I come into your life, I bring all the power of light. I bring not only illumination but also healing. Light heals. It irradiates bacteria, viruses, and fungi. Vitamin D—an essential element for healthy bodies—can only be produced by light. I irradiate sin's toxins, sooth painful soul wounds, and bring light to bear on hidden hurts. I am the Light of the World, but I am also *your* Light. Bask here.

"Where, except in uncreated light, can the darkness be drowned?"

—C. S. Lewis, *Letters to Malcolm*

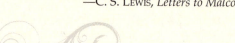

FEBRUARY 27
Child,

Do the thing in front of you. Don't worry ahead. Don't try to project the outcome. Just do the thing. You don't need to wait until your thoughts are aligned, or your emotions are right. Just do the thing. Don't try to *feel* faith, just *do* faith. Do what you need to do and everything else will meet you there.

"There's some task which the God of all the universe, the great Creator, your redeemer in Jesus Christ, has for you to do, and which will remain undone and incomplete until by faith and obedience you step into the will of God."

—Alan Redpath

FEBRUARY 28
Child,

I speak. It is My nature. I did not once speak, then retreat into silence. The first thing I revealed about Myself in Scripture is that I am a speaking God. I speak *to you*. I'm not speaking some new truth. I'm speaking eternal truth into your present moment. My word is as powerful and creative and transforming right now as it was when I spoke matter into being. Listen. Let your heart hear.

"The facts are that God is not silent, has never been silent. It is the nature of God to speak. The second Person of the Holy Trinity is called the Word."

—A. W. Tozer, *The Pursuit of God*

FEBRUARY 29
Child,

I see you caught in shame and guilt. It is My enemy's favorite ploy, to cripple you with regret, remind you of failure, bring up weakness. My Son died so you could be free of shame and guilt. Acknowledge your sin, repent, move on. It is not a spiritual exercise to mentally relive your sins and failures. All your sins are absorbed into My Son, and He bore them in His body on the Cross. (See 1 Peter 2:24.)

"[Grace] burst forth spontaneously from the bosom of eternal love, and rested not till it had removed every impediment, and found its way up to the sinner's side, swelling round him in full flow. It does away with the distance between the sinner and God, which sin had created. It meets the sinner on the spot where he stands; grace approaches him just as he is. [Grace] does not wait till there is something to attract it, nor till there is some good reason in the sinner for its flowing to him. . . . It was grace when it first thought of the sinner; it was grace when it found and laid hold of him; and it is grace still when it hands him up into glory."

—HORATIUS BONAR, *God's Purpose of Grace*

March

MARCH 1
Father,

I don't see the victory yet, but I know it is coming. You always and only lead me in triumph. Your plan is never for my defeat. Even though I am assailed on every side, even though it seems my circumstances are arrayed against me, today I begin a preemptive celebration. I celebrate the coming victory. I rejoice in God my Savior. I will not wallow in sorrow and declare defeat. You are my shield and my very great reward. I rejoice in You.

"The essence of optimism is not its view of the present, but the fact that it is the inspiration of life and hope when others give in; it enables a man to hold his head high when everything seems to be going wrong; it gives him strength to sustain reverses and yet claim the future for himself instead of abandoning it to his opponent."

—Dietrich Bonhoeffer

MARCH 2
Child,

Living in love is the most convincing evidence of My power in you. Love is not an emotion, but an action. It is rarely convenient. It requires that you set yourself aside and act with another's best interest in mind. Yet, it brings joy and peace into your life. Love is a paradox. It comes at a cost, but it adds to your life. Your act of love can be the healing balm for someone else's pain. Your loving response can be the very event that brings Me into the experience of another. Where before I might have been hearsay, through you I become proven fact. Today, watch for openings to be the demonstration of My love to someone else.

"Be devoted to one another in love. Honor one another above yourselves" (Romans 12:10).

MARCH 3
Father,

I find myself dismissing small opportunities to show love to those who are welded into my life—those loved ones who are the fixtures in my life. I tend to overlook the ordinary, everyday thinking that the deliberate expressions of love can be saved for the big junctures. I act as if love has to come in big, sweeping gestures. But my life is lived in small moments. Small exchanges, routine actions, repeated expressions. Move me to express love in these in-betweens. Teach me that every second I live affords me openings to express the love that comes from You through me. Let me live on alert, love at the ready.

"You can give without loving, but you cannot love without giving."
—AMY CARMICHAEL

MARCH 4
Child,

You are full of Christ. Full to overflowing. That fullness is not like a car filled with gasoline. You can't use it up or deplete it. You don't run low and need new supply. The Power that fills you is not a substance, or something I give apart from Myself. The Power that fills you is the person of Christ, brought into your experience by My Spirit. You always have all you need. You always have the fullness of Christ. You can block the free flow of His life through you by disobedience or sin, but you don't lose any of the fullness. Today, live in the fullness of Christ. Let Him flow freely.

"For in Christ all the fullness of the Deity lives in bodily form, and in Christ you have been brought to fullness" (COLOSSIANS 2:9–10).

"And I pray that you, being rooted and established in love, may have power, together with all the Lord's holy people, to grasp how wide and long and high and deep is the love of Christ, and to know this love that surpasses knowledge — that you may be filled to the measure of all the fullness of God" (Ephesians 3:17–19).

MARCH 5
Father,

The wait seems interminable. I don't see any end in sight. I see You work in other areas, and for other people, but in this You seem absent. But I know You are not absent or unconcerned. I know You are managing everything behind the scenes. Today, as I struggle with what I don't know, I will cling to what I do know. I know You are good. I know You are in charge. I know that You are strategic in Your ways and in Your timing. I know that You see the whole picture. I know that You are God.

"Never think that God's delays are God's denials. Hold on; hold fast; hold out. Patience is genius."

—Georges-Louis Leclerc, Comte de Buffon

MARCH 6
Child,

I know it seems that you are seeking Me, but it is just the opposite. I am seeking you. Your desire for Me is born of My desire for you. I am not hidden. I am not obscure. Your first leaning toward me was a response to My drawing you. When you hunger after Me, it means that I am knocking at your heart's door. Just open wide. I am here. Always, I am here.

"Here I am! I stand at the door and knock. If anyone hears my voice

and opens the door, I will come in and eat with that person, and they with me" (REVELATION 3:20).

MARCH 7
Father,

Today my heart's eyes gaze on You in the glory and majesty of heaven's throne room. To think that as You manage the universe, and as You receive Your rightful due—unending worship and adoration—You still have me on Your heart. You are attentive to even my sighs and groans. You know what's in my heart before it reaches my lips. You have met my needs before I know I have them. You make even my darkness light. Eternal God, King of the Universe, Almighty One . . . thinking about me.

"Before a word is on my tongue you, LORD, know it completely. You hem me in behind and before, and you lay your hand upon me. Such knowledge is too wonderful for me, too lofty for me to attain" (PSALM 139:4–6).

MARCH 8
Child,

I'm handling things. You can live with that as your touchstone. It will free you to follow Me wholeheartedly and without second-guessing. Listen to Me and do what I lead you to do. Go or stay, speak or be silent, act or be still based on what I say, not on what seems expedient at the moment. Rest in Me and trust that I can communicate My will and My wisdom to you. I know how to reach you, so just let Me be Me.

"What I am urging is simply that you become delightfully detached from the pressure of circumstance, so that it ceases to be the criterion

in the decisions you make. You do as you are told, whether God's instructions appear to be compatible with the immediate situation or not, and you leave God to vindicate Himself and to justify the course of action upon which you have embarked at His command."

—MAJOR W. IAN THOMAS, *The Indwelling Life of Christ*

MARCH 9
Child,

My call to you is framed so that it keeps you desperately dependent on My presence every moment. Hear your call in My call to Abraham: "Leave your country, your people and your father's household to the land I will show you" (Genesis 12:1). I don't give you a map with a starting point and an ending point and send you on your way. I call you to a journey, the path and destination of which only I know. At every step, you must be listening to Me. Will you follow Me step by step? "By faith Abraham, when called to go to a place he would later receive as his inheritance, obeyed and went, even though he did not know where he was going" (Hebrews 11:8).

"Have you been asking God what He is going to do? He will never tell you. God does not tell you what He is going to do—He reveals to you who He is."

—OSWALD CHAMBERS, *My Utmost for His Highest*

MARCH 10
Child,

Letting go of familiar is unsettling. The unknown feels risky. I'm not calling you to the unknown, but to Myself. Look at Me. I'm known. I have made Myself known to you through My Son and My Spirit and through My work in your life. You know Me.

I know the way and I know the destination and I know the good that waits for you in the place I'm leading you. You don't need to know, because I know.

"God's commands are, in the end, promises. He commands an obedience that will clear the way for His promised provision."
—JENNIFER KENNEDY DEAN, *Life Unhindered*

MARCH 11
Child,

When I call you *from*, I'm calling you *to*. I'm never depriving you of something good to give you something less. Where I'm calling you to let go, to leave behind, it is because I am calling you to the provision I have in place that you have not yet imagined. I have more for you. Ignore that part of you that wants to hang on to what you already know, and listen to that part of you that is craving more of Me.

"When it comes to the point of obedience to God's clear instructions, the Life of Jesus Christ within you makes human circumstances irrelevant; for to share His Life now as He once shared His Father's Life on earth is to know, as Jesus did, that Someone else is taking care of the consequences."
—MAJOR W. IAN THOMAS, *The Indwelling Life of Christ*

MARCH 12
Child,

Would you put yourself in My hands today to be a conduit for My healing in someone's life? Be observant and watchful. If you'll be on call, I'll bring hurting people into your path. They won't need a sermon, or a great and pious display. Just a touch or a smile or a kind word. In your daily rhythms, as you go about your activities, I'll use you to lift up and encourage and love. You might not even know when it happens, but an ordinary exchange in an ordinary setting can be My divine assignation. Just be ready.

"One of the principal rules of religion is, to lose no occasion of serving God. And, since he is invisible to our eyes, we are to serve him in our neighbour, which he receives as if done to himself in person standing visibly before us."

—JOHN WESLEY, *A Plain Account of Christian Perfection*

MARCH 13
Father,

Search my heart at the deepest places, and show me where my actions and thoughts are being dictated by my flesh instead of by Your Spirit. Probe those places where I'm feeling offended, hurt, taken for granted, unappreciated. What lies beneath? What underlying cause is producing these symptoms? I confess that I'm letting my own pride and self-focused responses keep me from being fully at Your disposal. I surrender those places that you have pinpointed and ask that You so fill me with Yourself that my pettiness is flooded out and washed away.

"Search me, God, and know my heart; test me and know my anxious thoughts. See if there is any offensive way in me, and lead me in the way everlasting" (PSALM 139:23–24).

MARCH 14
Child,

I have formed you and designed you so that, in every detail, you are who and how I need you to be for what I have called you to do. You are well thought out. The particular experiences you have walked through, the very struggles you have endured, your particular weaknesses, and your particular strengths—all of it. You are framed and arranged and constructed—inside and out—for My purpose. Stop wishing you were something else, or someone else, and yield all to Me. Watch what I can do.

"For you created my inmost being; you knit me together in my mother's womb. I praise you because I am fearfully and wonderfully made; your works are wonderful, I know that full well. My frame was not hidden from you when I was made in the secret place, when I was woven together in the depths of the earth. Your eyes saw my unformed body; all the days ordained for me were written in your book before one of them came to be" (Psalm 139:13–16).

MARCH 15
Child,

Before I reveal Myself *through* you, I first reveal Myself *in* you. My heavy lifting is the work I do in you to change you and make you into a vessel through which I can pour Myself into your world. You want My power operating through you in greater measure, but you resist the inner work that precedes it. Accept and receive the shaping work I'm doing in you. Uncomfortable circumstances, difficult situations, unmanageable people—all are My tools to do work *in* you that will result in power *through* you. Will you allow Me to work in you?

"But when God, who set me apart from my mother's womb and called me by his grace, was pleased to reveal his Son in *me so that I might preach him among the Gentiles, my immediate response was not to consult any human being"* (Galatians 1:15–16; author's emphasis).

MARCH 16

Father,

You are my strength. You are the source of anything good or strong about me. When I look anywhere else for vitality, I fall flat. Soak me with Your presence today. Let me marinate my life in Your word. My only need is You. My only goal is You. My only expectation is You.

"There are times when a Christian needs to lie still, like the earth under the spring rain, letting the lesson of experience and the memories of the Word of God sink down to the very roots of his life and fill the deep reservoirs of his soul."

—Mrs. Charles E. (L. B. E.) Cowman, *Springs in the Valley*

MARCH 17

Child,

Timing is everything. I am a God of timing. I act in fulfilled time, not elapsed time. Think of your time of waiting as a vessel I am filling full. When I have poured into it everything I intend, then the wait is over. Trust My timing. It is not random, but instead it is carefully calibrated.

"But let us also remember that delays are not refusals. Many a prayer is registered, and underneath it the words, 'My time is not yet come.' God has a set time as well as a set purpose, and He who orders the bounds of our habitation, orders also the time of our deliverance."

—Mrs. Charles E. (L. B. E.) Cowman, *Streams in the Desert*

MARCH 18
Father,

I have no need for which You do not have abundant supply. Your resources are never stretched, Your strength never strained. My fretting and worrying does nothing to improve the situation. It only diminishes me. Today I fix my eyes on those things only my heart can see. Today I let Your great supply define whatever I might call a "need." In light of Your riches, all my needs are already met.

"What a source—'God'! What a supply—'his glorious riches'! What a channel—'Christ Jesus'! It is your heavenly privilege to trust 'all your needs' to 'his glorious riches,' and to forget 'your needs' in the presence of 'his . . . riches.' In His great love, He has thrown open to you His exhaustive treasury. Go in and draw upon Him in simple childlike faith, and you will never again have the need to rely on anything else."

—Mrs. Charles E. (L. B. E.) Cowman

MARCH 19
Child,

Don't be surprised that you have difficulties and sorrows in life. Life is punctuated with sorrow. Believers and unbelievers alike. Both the good and the evil. No one escapes because it is the nature of this world. I do not promise you that you will have no sorrow. I promise this: you will experience only that which can be raw material for Me to use as I form you into a vessel for My honor. Only the challenges that will build you and not destroy you will ever enter your experience. Let Me use your struggles to accomplish in your life what could not be accomplished any other way.

"Thou canst not tell how rich a dowry sorrow gives the soul, how firm a faith and eagle sight of God."

—HENRY ALFORD

MARCH 20
Child,

I'm a pruner. "Every branch that does bear fruit he prunes so that it will be even more fruitful" (John 15:2–3). I cut away foliage that looks beautiful, but is instead a life-drain, clearing the way for more fruit. Sometimes the things you get most attached to, the things you are most proud of, are only taking up space where lasting fruit could be growing.

Be careful not to let exterior things define you and give you your sense of value. Family, career, possessions, friends, accomplishments, reputation. Not that there is anything wrong or sinful about any of these things, unless they get themselves wrapped around you so that you are captive to them. How will you know if something that is innocuous in itself has become a hindrance to more fruit? When you are forced to let them go. Then you find out how possessed of them you have become.

"So long as we are quietly at rest amid favourable and undisturbed surroundings, faith sleeps as an undeveloped sinew within us; a thread, a germ, an idea. But when we are pushed out from all these surroundings with nothing but God to look to, then faith grows suddenly into a cable, a monarch oak, a master-principle of the life."

—F. B. MEYER, *The Obedience of Faith*

MARCH 21
Child,

Learn to navigate disappointment. This world is not your home. Nothing here will fully satisfy you. New things will grow old. Nothing will be unmitigated good. Joyful things will have a less joyful aspect hidden in them. Nothing hoped and longed for will be as fulfilling as you expected it to be. These are not thoughts meant to discourage you or make you pessimistic, but to protect you. Don't expect from earthly origin what only heaven can give. So, don't be taken by surprise and live in disillusionment. Life is what it is. Embrace each circumstance for both its joy and its pain. I use both to mold you. When you embrace a realistic view of what this life will afford you, then you can be optimistic even about the disappointments. I will use them to hone real, deep, lasting joy—the kind heaven gives.

"The deep undertone of the world is sadness; a solemn bass, occurring at measured intervals, and heard through all other tones. Ultimately, all the strains of this world's music resolve themselves into that tone; and I believe that, rightly felt, the Cross, and the Cross alone, interprets the mournful mystery of life—the sorrow of the Highest, the Lord of life—the result of error and sin, but ultimately remedial, purifying and exalting."

—Frederick W. Robertson, *Well-springs of Wisdom: From the Writings of Frederick W. Robertson*

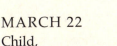

MARCH 22
Child,

You can count on this: whatever I want to show you, My enemy wants to obscure and blind you to. Anything My Spirit begins to formulate in your heart, the enemy will lie to you about. Big lies. Loud lies. Skillful lies. As soon as your heart begins to be stirred with My Spirit's whisper, "Things don't have to stay on the course they're on now," the enemy goes into action. "You? Of all people! You?" Or maybe, "Can you imagine how silly you'll look when you fail? You'll embarrass God!" Recognize that if the enemy weren't threatened by what your heart can see—like the pharaoh was threatened by the Israelites—then he wouldn't be doing all he could to distract you and bully you. If what you were about to obey were inconsequential, or off the mark, he'd be cheering you on. Ignore the enemy and his lies. Cling to Me and My voice.

"I was not disobedient to the vision from heaven" (Act 26:19).

MARCH 23
Child,

I have placed you exactly where I want you on this day. Be present to this day. This day has a call. It has a purpose. You don't have to scurry around and try to find it. My purpose will find you if you live your life alert to My Spirit. Keep your heart synchronized to Mine.

"This is the day that the Lord has made; let us rejoice and be glad in it" (Psalm 188:24 ESV).

MARCH 24
Child,

You think of yourself as obscure and the obedience I'm calling you to today as small and unimportant. But I never call you to an obedience that doesn't matter, and no citizen of My kingdom is obscure. How might Moses' mother have felt, do you think—just a little mom in a sea of moms, one of the nameless slaves in the exodus story? Likely no one would have picked Moses' mother out as the key to Israel's escape from Egypt and central to Israel's possessing the Promised Land. Are you amazed at how I work unnoticed in the most seemingly mundane situations, through the most obscure people? Abram of Ur. Jochebed of Egypt. Mary of Nazareth. I called Moses' mother to do one thing: build an ark of bulrushes. I'm calling you to do one thing: start right now building what I have called you to build. Everything starts small. Build it in obscurity and let Me decide when to set it afloat. Build in obedience, with no goal but to be obedient to the heavenly vision (Acts 26:19). Don't build it to own it; build it to let it go.

"If you know that God loves you, you should never question a directive from Him. It will always be right and best. When He gives you a directive, you are not just to observe it, discuss it, or debate it. You are to obey it."

—HENRY BLACKABY

MARCH 25
Child,

I want you free. Every command I give is meant to lead you into more freedom. When I command you to forgive, it is My loving call to you to walk in freedom. Unforgiveness keeps you tied to your past and keeps you tied to your offender. You carry your offender around on your back as a heavy, paralyzing load. When I died for the sins you have committed, I also died for the sins committed against you. Let Me pour My love into your heart. My love is big enough and powerful enough to dissolve anger and resentment—for your sake.

"And hope does not put us to shame, because God's love has been poured out into our hearts through the Holy Spirit, who has been given to us" (ROMANS 5:5).

MARCH 26
Father,

You forgive me so freely and so readily. The least infraction meets with Your immediate grace, and the gravest sin is absolved with prepaid atonement. I never have to earn my way back into Your favor. I never have to pay for my sins. I'm not expected to deserve the grace lavished on me. I hate my sins because they no longer fit me. I fear the chaos my sins bring to my life and the interruption of the free flow between You and me. But I don't have to fear Your retribution. I don't have to fear that You will walk away from my life. Empower me to forgive others as You forgive me—freely and readily.

"Forgive one another as quickly and thoroughly as God in Christ forgave you" (EPHESIANS 4:31–32 THE MESSAGE).

MARCH 27
Child,

Sometimes the obedience I am calling you to is inaction instead of action. It goes against your every fleshly instinct. You feel you must jump in and fix and manage everything to your prescripted conclusion. You feel you know exactly what needs to happen, and that you should, therefore, make it happen. But My command to you is to stay out of My way. It might be the hardest thing you've ever done. Pray, and watch Me work.

"I have to imagine that for many Hebrew warriors, all the marching and ram's horn blowing felt pretty silly. Surely some of them questioned the wisdom of the plan. They must have felt vulnerable and exposed to the enemy. I can imagine one of these battle-tested

warriors telling his story later and saying something like, 'The hardest thing I've ever done is not do what I've always done.'"

—Jennifer Kennedy Dean, *Life Unhindered!*

MARCH 28

Jesus,

Fill me so full of Yourself that You take up all the space. Nothing but You. No room for flesh's ways, or sin's pull. All the places of pettiness and selfishness that occupy my life, I surrender them to You for cleansing. Wash me and I will be whiter than snow.

"What heavens are laid up in Jesus! What rivers of infinite bliss have their source, ay, and every drop of their fullness in Him! Since, O sweet Lord Jesus, Thou art the present portion of Thy people, favor us this year with such a sense of Thy preciousness, that from its first to its last day, we may be glad and rejoice in Thee."

—C. H. Spurgeon, *Morning and Evening: Daily Readings*

MARCH 29

Jesus,

I require a continual inflow of You in my life. Because You have called me to let You live through me, it is not a life I can replenish. It requires You, always pouring Yourself in me so You can pour Yourself out through me. I'm like a tree planted by rivers of water. The flowing water always nourishes my roots. The trees take in the water through their roots, letting it circulate to every cell and molecule. The water that once flowed in the river now flows in the trees. The fruit the trees bear season after season is the visible evidence of what we don't see—strong root systems. Without You, I die.

"That person is like a tree planted by streams of water, which yields its fruit in season and whose leaf does not wither—whatever they do prospers" (PSALM 1:3).

MARCH 30
Child,

You are not a cistern, to be filled with water from an outside source and then left spent and emptied, as if the water had never been. Instead, I have designed you to be a fountain, with a source deep inside that never runs dry. The water that flows from you is living, moving, powerful, gushing from a continual supply. Let the fountain of My life bubble up in you, and you will not be able to hold back its force. The Living Water will make His own way through you into your world.

"Whoever drinks the water I give them will never thirst. Indeed, the water I give them will become in them a spring of water welling up to eternal life" (JOHN 4:14).

MARCH 31
Jesus,

The more I know You, the more I long for those around me to experience the You that I experience. I want You to flow from me in the same power You flow through me. Teach me how to stay in Your flow so that what comes from me is what has come through You. Call me back when I look elsewhere to quench my thirst. Let my thirst for You grow until it is my sole occupation—to assuage my never-ending longing for You. Until You are the centerpiece of every thought I think. Until You are the author of every word I speak. Let me be the conduit for You into my world.

"'Let anyone who is thirsty come to me and drink. Whoever believes in me, as Scripture has said, rivers of living water will flow from within them.' By this he meant the Spirit, whom those who believed in him were later to receive" (JOHN 7:37–39).

April

APRIL 1
Child,

I've given you My Son—first *for* you, then *in* you. The culmination of the great salvation I worked out for you is that Christ is in you. Everything I have is housed in Him, and He is housed in you. Everything you need is on deposit in you. Just let Him flow. Don't block Him by your disobedience. Step out of His way, and let Him do what only He can do.

"Our blessed Jesus, as God, is omniscient, omnipresent, omnipotent. Will it not console you to know that all these great and glorious attributes are altogether yours? Has He power? That power is yours to support and strengthen you, to overcome your enemies, and to preserve you even to the end. Has He love? Well, there is not a drop of love in His heart which is not yours; you may dive into the immense ocean of His love, and you may say of it all, 'It is mine.'"
—Charles Spurgeon, *Morning and Evening: Daily Readings*

APRIL 2
Father,

I choose to rest in You. Instead of striving and toiling and trying to figure everything out, I choose to rest in You. I know You will reveal what I need to know when I need to know it. I know that Your wisdom is available to me at exactly the instant I need it. I know that You will put the right supply in my life at the right time and in the right way. I lay my concerns at Your feet and rest in You. You have given me Christ, who fills everything in every way (Ephesians 1:23). I can rest.

"All things belong to you, and you belong to Christ; and Christ belongs to God" (1 Corinthians 3:21–23 NASB).

APRIL 3
Child,

I have loved you with an everlasting love. Before you knew Me, I knew you. I planned you. I designed you. I delighted in creating you. You are an expression of My highest creativity. I love to point to you and say to My angels, "Look what I made!" I look at you and you bring Me joy. I know every single thing about you, and I adore you. I see what you are becoming, not just what you are. Today, don't fall for the old subterfuge that My enemy tries to trick you with—that you are a disappointment to Me, that I'm angry with you. I see the flaws. I'm not looking through rose-colored glasses and overlooking your sins. But I see past them. I see where those very weaknesses will be the places My strength will be most obvious. I see beyond your now. And I cherish you unequivocally, without a caveat of any sort. I just love you.

"My frame was not hidden from you when I was made in the secret place, when I was woven together in the depths of the earth. Your eyes saw my unformed body; all the days ordained for me were written in your book before one of them came to be" (PSALM 139:15–16).

APRIL 4
Child,

I see your yearning over the life of that one whom you love, and whose heart's condition is a sorrow to you. You feel helpless and hopeless. No truth seems to penetrate the lie. No light seems to pierce the darkness. But I assure you that no matter what you observe from your vantage place on earth, it looks very different from where I'm sitting. Your dear one is no mystery to Me. I know what you don't. I know where in that one's heart the lie is lodged.

I know how the lie got a toehold there. And, I know how to bring light to bear exactly where the darkness resides. Trust Me. I'm working. Just let Me do what only I can do. Your dear one cannot hide from Me. You pray, releasing all My power and provision into your loved one's life and let Me do the work.

"Where can I go from your Spirit? Where can I flee from your presence? If I go up to the heavens, you are there; if I make my bed in the depths, you are there. If I rise on the wings of the dawn, if I settle on the far side of the sea, even there your hand will guide me, your right hand will hold me fast. If I say, 'Surely the darkness will hide me and the light become night around me,' even the darkness will not be dark to you; the night will shine like the day, for darkness is as light to you" (PSALM 139:7–12).

APRIL 5
Child,

I love broken people. I use broken people. Broken people are the only ones My life can flow freely from. I have put you into relationship with exactly those whose lives will be enriched by the work I do in you and through your broken places. I call you to be a container and dispenser of My life. You are a clay jar, and I am the Living Water that fills it. Nothing fancy about a clay jar. Nothing impressive. Nothing to call attention. The WOW! factor is found in what the jar contains. When you can be "hard pressed . . . but not crushed; perplexed, but not in despair; persecuted, but not abandoned; struck down, but not destroyed" (2 Corinthians 4:8–9)—then you will be a container and dispenser of a power not your own. When there is nothing that looks like power, but power comes through anyway—it is clearly an all-surpassing power that is from Me and not from you.

"But we have this treasure in jars of clay to show that this all-surpassing power is from God and not from us. We are hard pressed

on every side, but not crushed; perplexed, but not in despair; persecuted, but not abandoned; struck down, but not destroyed" (2 Corinthians 4:7–9).

APRIL 6
Child,

My broken and fractured jar of clay, My cracked vessel. As Living Water pours in, it pours out through your broken places. As long as Living Water is pouring in, then Living Water is pouring out. If My goal were a pot to hold Water in, then you would not be a good choice. But My goal is to pour Water out, and you are perfect for My purposes. Turn a broken pot on its side and look in. All dark. Except for the broken places. That's where the light shines through. Your brokenness is beautiful to Me and more useful to Me than perfection could ever be.

"'My grace is sufficient for you, for my power is made perfect in weakness.' Therefore I will boast all the more gladly about my weaknesses, so that Christ's power may rest on me. That is why, for Christ's sake, I delight in weaknesses, in insults, in hardships, in persecutions, in difficulties. For when I am weak, then I am strong" (2 Corinthians 12:9–10).

APRIL 7
Child,

You're looking in the wrong place. Your attention is on your need, and it looms large. Next, you evaluate your ability, and it is paltry. But lift your eyes. Look at Me. I am not troubled. I am not stymied. I am not at a loss. Look at Me. Fix your gaze here. I am your answer.

"Many Christians estimate difficulty in the light of their own resources, and thus they attempt very little, and they always fail. All giants have been weak men who did great things for God because they reckoned on His power and presence to be with them."

—HUDSON TAYLOR

APRIL 8
Father,

I'm all out of words. I've said them all. I've said every word I know to say, and I'm tired. So, here I am. The only words I have left to say are, "Daddy! Daddy!"

"Did any of you, parents, ever hear your child wake from sleep with some panic fear, and shriek the mother's name through the darkness? Was not that a more powerful appeal than all words? And, depend upon it, that the soul which cries aloud on God, 'the God and Father of our Lord Jesus 'Christ,' though it have 'no language but a cry,' will never call in vain."

—ALEXANDER MACLAREN, "A PATTERN OF PRAYER,"
Sermons Preached in Manchester: Third Series

APRIL 9
Child,

I can read your heart. When words no longer express what your heart feels, I know what you mean. When words seem vapid and worthless compared to the great cry of your heart, I understand. Don't struggle so for words that you might say to Me. Let Me say My words to you. You'll find that My words are spirit and life. You'll find that My voice awakens new thoughts. Before a word is on your tongue, I have heard it fully. When you have nothing but sighs and groans, I hear it as if you had spoken it perfectly. You have no words left? Don't lose heart. I am full of words.

"Before a word is on my tongue you, Lord, know it completely" (Psalm 139:4).

APRIL 10
Child,

You're walking through some deep waters. Rest assured that this is your path. You are not walking in the deep by accident. I have always known that your path would cross these waters. You're strong enough. I made sure you were ready before this leg of your pilgrimage came into view. I will show you realities about Myself that you will not learn any other way. You will see Me as you have not seen Me before. When you get to the other side of this jaunt, it will have been worth it. Trust Me in this.

"When you pass through the waters, I will be with you; and when you pass through the rivers, they will not sweep over you. When you walk through the fire, you will not be burned; the flames will not set you ablaze. For I am the Lord your God, the Holy One of Israel, your Savior" (Isaiah 43:2–3).

APRIL 11
Jesus,

I thirst for You as if I am in a dry and thirsty land. I feel that I must know Your presence to be with me in this quiet hour. You are my heart's desire. You are my soul's hiding place. Nothing else will do. I bring my life to you and lay it out at Your feet like the lame man on his mat (Luke 5:19). I'm here, in all my neediness. Touch me.

"His hand can cool the heat of my burning brow, and calm the tumult of my palpitating heart. That glorious right hand which moulded the world can new-create my mind; the unwearied hand which bears the earth's huge pillars up can sustain my spirit. The loving hand which encloses all the saints can cherish me; and the mighty hand that breaks in pieces the enemy can subdue my sins. Why should I not feel that hand touching me this evening?"

—CHARLES SPURGEON, *Morning and Evening: Daily Readings*

APRIL 12
Child,

Let Me show you what I see when I look at you. I know what you see. You see every speck of grime, every imagined disfigurement, every conceived imperfection. You think that's how I see you. You think that your flaws surely would repulse one as beautiful and holy as I am. But I see you dressed in Christ. I see you covered by His righteousness. When I look at you, I am filled with love. I am blinded by your beauty. Look through My eyes. See your own loveliness. Believe My estimation. Let Me be your mirror.

"How beautiful you are and how pleasing, my love, with your delights!" (SONG OF SONGS 7:6).

APRIL 13
Child,

Don't worry about the future. Don't look into the unknown and let fear settle in. Your unknown is not unknown to Me. I know what lies ahead, and knowing means that I have prepared for it. Instead of letting your thoughts linger on what you don't know, consider what you do know. Rest your thoughts on My unchangeable truth. I am faithful and trustworthy. You know that. Rest there.

"Nothing but Christian faith gives to the furthest future the solidity and definiteness which it must have if it is to be a breakwater for us against the fluctuating sea of present cares and thoughts."
—Alexander Maclaren, *Expositions of Holy Scripture: Genesis, Exodus, Leviticus and Numbers*

APRIL 14
Child,

My grace is sufficient for any situation. Never will there be a circumstance that can overwhelm My grace. But I do not give grace for your imagination about what might happen. When you look into your future and imagine grim and terrible happenings, there is no grace for that. I have all the grace you need when you need it. Don't waste your emotions imagining a future that will likely never come.

"I can do all this through him who gives me strength" (Philippians 4:13).

APRIL 15
Child,

With your mind's eye, look at My cross. Blood-soaked, rough hewn, jagged, there is nothing sweet or pretty here. Crucifixion is a savage death. Stand with Me here at the foot of My cross. Consider it. Reach out and touch it. Feel its texture. Contemplate My love for you that held Me to the terrible cross so that you would not have to bear the weight of your own sin. It has been some time since you have let the wonder of the Cross settle on you. Take some time now and let the old truth come to you as if freshly heard.

"At the heart of the story stands the cross of Christ where evil did its worst and met its match."

—JOHN W. WENHAM

APRIL 16
Jesus,

The Cross was Your choice. You did not romanticize it, but looked at it clear-eyed and saw all its horror and chose it anyway. Let my heart wrap itself around that fact and never let go. We—little worthless sinners—are of such value to You that, for us, You laid down Your life of Your own choice.

"But God demonstrates his own love for us in this: While we were still sinners, Christ died for us" (ROMANS 5:8).

APRIL 17
Child,

I hate sin because I love you. Sin diminishes you and hinders you and wounds you. My warning away from sin is from a bottomless well of passionate love. To see how much I hate sin, you need only look at the Cross. To see how much I love you, you need only look at the Cross.

"By the cross we know the gravity of sin and the greatness of God's love toward us."

—JOHN CHRYSOSTOM

APRIL 18
Child,

As you stand at the Cross, in your mind's eye, it becomes the place where you offer yourself as a living offering to Me. Today, as you are in My presence and at the foot of My cross, offer yourself. Past, present, future. Disappointments, wounds, betrayals. Successes, victories, joys. Possessions, relationships, positions. Everything My Spirit names to you, offer it for My use. Let Me use everything about your life in My service. Spend enough time to let Me have My say in every area of your life. Let time be your gift to Me today.

"Offer yourselves to God as those who have been brought from death to life; and offer every part of yourself to him as an instrument of righteousness" (ROMANS 6:13).

APRIL 19
Father,

My little boat is being tossed all over. The storm is raging, and You have not commanded it to cease. I feel very windswept and exposed right now. But I know You are in this boat with me. I know You have the say about how long this storm can last and how much it can throw my boat around. If You are in this with me, and the storm is still raging, then I trust that the waves and the wind are carrying me to a destination You have in mind. I trust myself to Your presence, and let the winds roar.

"Right now I am storm-tossed. And what am I going to say? 'Father, get me out of this'? No, this is why I came in the first place. I'll say, 'Father, put your glory on display'" (JOHN 12:27–28 THE MESSAGE).

APRIL 20
Child,

I am determined to deliver all of Jesus into your life and circumstances. Some have pictured Me as a polite Guest, waiting quietly to be noticed. I am neither passive nor polite. I am intrusive, demanding, and stubborn because My love for you drives Me. I don't give up. You can quench My Spirit. You can grieve My Spirit. You can ignore My voice. But you can't make Me give up on you. I will pursue your heart, and I will wrestle you until I win you. Love never surrenders.

"This is love: not that we loved God, but that he loved us and sent his Son as an atoning sacrifice for our sins" (1 John 4:10).

APRIL 21
Child,

Because I want you free, My enemy wants you bound. He has targeted your freedom and works against it with energy and craftiness. He strategizes how best to limit and steal your freedom. Look around your life. Where are you doing what you don't want to do? Where are you responding in ways that take you captive to anger and resentment and limit your joy? Where are you caught up in pretense and pretending and hiding your reality from others? Where are you blinded to others because you have become the center of your focus? All these are the enemy's well-practiced game plan for how to sideline you and keep you from full effect for the kingdom. Don't fall for it. Recognize it for what it is, and resist in the power of My Spirit. "No, in the name of Jesus," is a powerful statement as you recognize the enemy's ploys seeking to suck you in.

"If you hold to my teaching, you are really my disciples. Then you will know the truth, and the truth will set you free" (John 8:31–32).

APRIL 22
Child,

I am a present God. Not just a god of past deeds. Not just a god of history. I am fully present in your life right now with the same power, authority, and love as I displayed in times past. For Me, past is always present and future is always present. I am a present God. In your circumstance, on this day, at this hour I Am.

"In the context of your present circumstances, God's name is a present-tense name. Not I WAS. Not I WILL BE. His name is always I AM. Do you see that by telling you that His name is I AM it changes the center of gravity of the whole relationship? Everything tips in His direction. The burdens, the expectations, the pressure to perform, the disappointments all roll off your shoulders and land at His feet. Everything changes for you when you have encountered your I AM."
—Jennifer Kennedy Dean, *Power in the Name of Jesus*

APRIL 23
Child,

When you speak the name of Jesus, you are speaking the most precious, costly word in all creation. You are speaking the word that thrills heaven and demoralizes hell. When the name of Jesus crosses your lips, all the power of heaven is set in motion on your behalf. It is the only word you need to know. It says all there is to be said.

"Therefore God exalted him to the highest place and gave him the name that is above every name, that at the name of Jesus every knee

should bow, in heaven and on earth and under the earth, and every tongue acknowledge that Jesus Christ is Lord, to the glory of God the Father" (PHILIPPIANS 2:9–11).

APRIL 24
Child,

You have enough faith. Faith's focus is Me, not an outcome. When you have enough faith to turn to Me, no matter the state of your feelings, then you have enough faith. Tell Me about your weak and wobbly faith. Only I can remedy it. Trying to chase doubt from your heart is a useless exercise. Just don't let your enemy convince you that you cannot come to Me until all your doubts have been erased and you can bring Me perfect faith. The tiniest spark of faith is enough faith to activate all My power on your behalf.

"Truly I tell you, if you have faith as small as a mustard seed, you can say to this mountain, 'Move from here to there,' and it will move. Nothing will be impossible for you" (MATTHEW 17:20).

APRIL 25
Child,

I give impossible visions. If it were possible, it would be an assignment or a project—but it is vision. When vision takes shape on the earth, there will be no doubt about Whose vision it is. I will implant vision in you that only I can bring into being. Don't try to scale back what I have spoken into the deep places of your heart. Don't try to make it fit what you can do. When you scale back or water down My vision, you are not "[taking] hold of that for which Christ Jesus took hold of [you]" (Philippians 3:12). I will not bring about a diluted form of My vision. If what you are envisioning about a situation negates or underestimates My power, you are limiting Me to only what you can imagine.

"We have this treasure in jars of clay to show that this all-surpassing power is from God and not from us" (2 CORINTHIANS 4:7).

APRIL 26
Child,

The call that I have placed in your life, the vision that I have implanted in your heart, is also a promise. I will bring it about. I will provide for every need in relation to the call. I will provide your passion, your insight, your clear understanding. I will open every door, give the necessary finances, provide what you need when you need it as you walk out the call, always listening to My voice.

"And God is able to make all grace abound to you, so that in all things at all times, having all that you need, you will abound in every good work" (2 CORINTHIANS 9:8).

APRIL 27
Father,

I can't see what You're doing. I can't imagine how this small moment in my small life makes much difference to the grand scheme. But You won't relent. You keep reminding me, and impressing me, and making me restless. No one else will know whether I obey You in this or not. It will be between You and me. I surrender to this humbling obedience that seems insignificant because it is You who calls me.

"Sometimes we are called to small, even perhaps humbling, moments

of obedience. Obedience that calls on us to die to all pride and embrace the power of small. In the moment, it is hard to believe that God designed this, or that it could be elevated in any way. We can't extrapolate from the small obedience what grand outcome it might have, but we can know by faith that every obedience matters. It might be grooming us, or giving us needed experience, or simply conquering flesh that is fed by pride. But it matters."

—JENNIFER KENNEDY DEAN, *The Power of Small: Think Small to Live Large*

APRIL 28
Father,

Right now, it feels to me like You are more intent on taking away than giving. Instead of seeing great provision roll in, I'm watching small provision get smaller. Yet the vision won't abate. Your Spirit keeps breathing life into the vision You have caused me to see in my innermost being. The call stays strong, and the vision big, but the resources dwindle. This is Your doing. I trust that You know how to manage this situation. I know You have a bigger agenda than I do, and that You are working at every level all the time. So, I choose today to trust You, and if taking away resources is how You are multiplying my faith, I'm all in.

"Gideon's 10,000 became 300. Supplies were being taken away, and faith was growing stronger. Funny how that works. The old, small Gideon had become Gideon, the mighty warrior. The Gideon who had defined himself as too small and insignificant for the call had learned the power of a Big God. So, when the Lord gave him the battle plan—the puny little battle plan that entailed trumpets and empty jars and torches—he didn't bat an eye. He was ready to take on the whole enemy's army and pit his small against their big."

—JENNIFER KENNEDY DEAN, *The Power of Small: Think Small to Live Large*

APRIL 29
Child,

Suffuse your life with thanksgiving and marinate your heart in praise. I'm not talking about the kind of praise and thanksgiving that seems in line with events. I'm saying to wrap everything in thanksgiving, especially when the situation would seem to call for anxiety and worry.

"Do not be anxious about anything, but in everything, by prayer and petition, with thanksgiving, present your requests to God. And the peace of God, which transcends all understanding, will guard your hearts and your minds in Christ Jesus" (PHILIPPIANS 4:6–7).

APRIL 30
Child,

Praise is your best weapon. Something supernaturally powerful happens when you walk in praise. It reorients your thoughts and resets your emotions. I don't remind you to praise Me at all times because I'm a needy, narcissistic God, but because you need it. It strips the enemy of his most potent mechanism— dissatisfaction. It overturns fear and causes faith to sprout. You can't overdo praise.

"People who have learned the value of praise and thanksgiving are fortified and ready for whatever life brings. But you learn it in the small things. That's where you integrate it into your life so that it is your default mode. It's like learning a foreign language. You have to practice it and immerse yourself in it until it is so much a part of you that you even think in your new vocabulary of praise."
—JENNIFER KENNEDY DEAN, *The Power of Small: Think Small to Live Large*

May

MAY 1
Child,

The absolute certainty of My love is the glue that holds everything together. It is the one thing that makes sense of life, and the reality that defines all other reality. The promise of My unfailing love anchors the heart, no matter what. Here is a promise that can burrow into the depths of your heart and make a home there: I will never forget you, abandon you, or fail you. You are so precious to Me that you are never out of My thoughts; you are never left out in the cold.

"Let your faith in Christ, the Omnipresent One, be in the quiet confidence that He will be with you every day and every moment. Meet Him in prayer, and let His presence be your strength for service."

—ANDREW MURRAY, *Teach Me to Pray*

MAY 2
Child,

You are busy trying to arrange outward events in such a way that they will produce inward contentment—a sense of safety, of being loved, of satisfaction. If this would happen, or if that would go away, or if this would change, or if that would stay the same, you think, *Then I would have inner contentment.* Learn that it's not what I do, but who I am that produces contentment. What happened on the outside of you does not add to or subtract from your inner peace.

"You will keep in perfect peace those whose minds are steadfast, because they trust in you. Trust in the LORD forever, for the LORD, the LORD himself, is the Rock eternal" (ISAIAH 26:3–4).

MAY 3
Child

You are My friend. That's right—friend. I let you in on My private thoughts. I delight in back-and-forth conversation with you. We can communicate with just a wink, or a nod. We have a shorthand language between us because you are My friend. You're an insider. I let you in on My plans, and I share insider information with you. Today, live in the glow of our friendship.

"I no longer call you servants, because a servant does not know his master's business. Instead, I have called you friends, for everything that I learned from my Father I have made known to you" (JOHN 15:15).

MAY 4
Child,

When you receive criticism, I know it hurts your feelings. That's fine. But don't reject it out of hand. Don't get so caught up in defending your pride that you miss something I might be trying to show you. Receive it humbly. Don't internalize criticism, but do sort through it for any kernel of truth. It may reveal to you that you are coming across to others in a way you don't intend. Or it may reveal something you don't see in yourself. Let Me use any criticism for your good, and let Me separate out for you what is valuable in it.

"Instruct the wise and they will be wiser still; teach the righteous and they will add to their learning" (PROVERBS 9:9).

MAY 5
Jesus,

My heart hears You calling me to follow You. I am drawn by that call. The words burn inside me and set me aflame with desire to be fully present to You and to be smack-dab in the middle of anything You're doing. I hear the call not as a command to a task, but as an invitation to a relationship. The closer I get to You, the closer I want to be. You're like superglue to my heart. Wherever I touch You, I am gripped. The more I know You, the more I cling to You. Jesus, teach me to follow You fully.

"Looking unto Jesus is at the same time a looking away from everything else."

— Erich Sauer (1898–1959), German theologian and writer

MAY 6
Father,

Today I find myself captivated by the reality of Your cleansing life flowing through me. Like blood flows through my body and washes away waste and toxins, You flow through me and wash away my sins and my unrighteousness. I'm savoring the feeling of being clean, because of You.

"Jesus has a way of seeing past secondary problems right to the heart of a matter. The [paralytic man on his mat] had a bigger problem than his paralysis, and Jesus responded to the disease, not the symptom. I have heard some speculate that the man must have been very disappointed to have been expecting to be healed, only to hear that his sins were forgiven. But I believe that in those words, this man received more than he had imagined or thought to ask for. The

healing of his legs must have seemed anticlimactic. Who would have imagined that Jesus could touch someone and wash that person clean on the inside?"

—Jennifer Kennedy Dean from *The One Year Praying the Promises of God* by Cheri Fuller and Jennifer Kennedy Dean

MAY 7

Child,

I have provided enough for this day. Don't reach into tomorrow and try to live tomorrow on today's strength. Embrace this day and its provision. You don't have what you need for tomorrow? It's not tomorrow yet.

"When the dew settled on the camp at night, the manna also came down" (Numbers 11:9).

MAY 8

Child,

Let Me shape your heart. Become soft, pliable, and moldable in My hands. I'm applying heat through some circumstances, but it is not to scorch you; rather it is to soften you. To make you transformable, trust Me, relinquish. Let Me work. Seek Me for what I will do *in* you, not just what I will do *for* you.

"Faith does not grasp a doctrine but a heart. The trust which Christ requires is the bond that unites souls with Him; and the very life of it is entire committal of myself to Him in all my relations and for all my needs, and absolute utter confidence in Him as all-sufficient for everything that I can require."

—Alexander Maclaren, *The Holy of Holies: Sermons on the Fourteenth, Fifteenth, and Sixteenth Chapters of the Gospel of John*

MAY 9
Father,

I long for Your Spirit to open Your Word to my deepest understanding. I know that the riches stored in the secret places are not sitting on the surface to be skimmed off by a casual observer. I know that Your Holy Spirit, who knows all the deep things of God, must reveal the depths of Your Word to me. I give You my mind and my intellect and my understanding and ask that You speak deep to me.

"The Spirit searches all things, even the deep things of God" (1 CORINTHIANS 2:10).

MAY 10
Child,

You've stepped out in response to My call, and now you find yourself in a raging storm. Everything seems set against you. Every circumstance seems to be buffeting you instead of moving you forward. Remember what I said in the beginning, when I first called you out. I will get you where you're going. Don't let the storm be your focus. Instead, let the words that launched you be the focus. Don't let the storm suck you in. Instead of being overwhelmed with the storm, you can be at rest with Me.

"That day when evening came, he said to his disciples, 'Let us go over to the other side.' Leaving the crowd behind, they took him along, just as he was, in the boat. There were also other boats with him. A furious squall came up, and the waves broke over the boat, so that it was nearly swamped. Jesus was in the stern, sleeping on a cushion" (MARK 4:35–38).

MAY 11
Child,

I have declared you to be holy. Don't cringe at that. Holiness doesn't mean that you will have to become stern and stoic. Holy means set aside for My purposes. It means to be taken out of use for any purpose other than Mine. Because you are holy, I'm training you to be holy in your thoughts and behavior so that your behavior matches your identity. That is the key to peace.

"I am the LORD your God; consecrate yourselves and be holy, because I am holy" (LEVITICUS 11:44).

MAY 12
Child,

Words are powerful weapons, either to build up or to tear down. Your words can live in the soul of another, either wounding and scarring, or healing and restoring. Wield words carefully. Let your words be informed by My Word. Let My Spirit deposit My words in your heart to come through your mouth. Don't use them carelessly.

"The mouth of the righteous is a fountain of life" (PROVERBS 10:11).

MAY 13
Jesus,

Nothing rivals the delight that knowing You brings into my life. I think about the things I thought I had to have in order to be happy or fulfilled. Some of those things I have achieved. They did not produce the lasting fulfillment I expected from them. Some of those things have never materialized, and I don't miss them. My desire for them disappeared as I matured in You. Just You. You are all I desire. Anything You bring into my life, I will enjoy as gifts from Your hand, but I won't look to them for my happiness. What You choose to withhold, I will not imagine would make me happy if only I could possess them. Just You, all I need.

"Whom have I in heaven but you? And earth has nothing I desire besides you. My flesh and my heart may fail, but God is the strength of my heart and my portion forever" (PSALM 73:25–26).

MAY 14
Child,

Before any scheme of My enemy reaches you, it has been weighed and measured by Me, and I have filtered from it anything that would destroy you, allowing only that which will enrich you. If the glory it will produce outweighs the pain it will cause, that is what I allow. Before you know what difficulties are headed your way, I know. My Son has already prayed for you. I have already answered His prayer. When you are hit with an unexpected heartache, you will walk into it fully prepared. Be assured, you will emerge from it better and richer than before it hit.

"Simon, Simon, Satan has asked to sift all of you as wheat. But I have prayed for you, Simon, that your faith may not fail. And when you have turned back, strengthen your brothers" (LUKE 22:31–32).

MAY 15

Child,

Consider what it means that you belong to Christ, who belongs to Me. All things are yours. Now. When you need them. I own and manage everything and you are Mine. You are My child. My beloved. You don't have to convince Me to come up with what you need. I don't have to figure out how to squeeze what you need out of My budget. It's already yours. I distribute it to you in line with My wisdom and My great love for you. But you are never without.

"All things belong to you, and you belong to Christ; and Christ belongs to God" (1 CORINTHIANS 3:22–23 NASB).

MAY 16

Child,

When I claim your life, I claim all of your life. No set-asides. No "everything but this." Time, money, talents, relationships, possessions—you are all Mine. I plan to use all of your life for kingdom purposes. You need to hold everything loosely. Let everything about your life be ready for Me to call it into service at any time. That is the adventure of walking with Me. Live ready.

"This is how you are to eat it: with your cloak tucked into your belt, your sandals on your feet and your staff in your hand." (EXODUS 12:11).

MAY 17

Child,

I am mighty to save. In the middle of your everyday comings and goings, look for Me. In the mundane and the ordinary, there I am. I am always striding toward you. You never have to search in vain for Me. I am always where You can see Me if you look. Little things, big things, in-between things—I'm mighty to save. Nothing too small for My attention and nothing too big for My power. In every setting and in every situation I'm the same— mighty to save.

"Who is this, robed in splendor, striding forward in the greatness of his strength? 'It is I, proclaiming victory, mighty to save'" (ISAIAH 63:1).

MAY 18
Child,

I will never let you sink. If you step out and then find yourself going under, I will immediately pull you up. My help is always a reach away. I don't lecture you about what you should have done or how you should have done it. I just put out My strong right hand and pull you to safety.

"But when he saw the wind, he was afraid and, beginning to sink, cried out, 'Lord, save me!' Immediately Jesus reached out his hand and caught him" (MATTHEW 14:30–31).

MAY 19
Child,

I have provided you with every weapon necessary to defeat your enemy in the spiritual realm. You enemy is spiritual and your weapons are spiritual. You weapons are not of this world— they do not wear out, misfire, or become obsolete. Your enemy has only one weapon: lies. You have the one weapon that will jam up the enemy's arsenal and cause his weapon to malfunction at the start. You have the Truth. His name is Jesus.

"The weapons we fight with are not the weapons of the world. On the contrary, they have divine power to demolish strongholds" (2 Corinthians 10:4–5).

MAY 20
Child,

It is My nature to give. I am more ready to give than you are to ask. I am not put off by your continual asking. I invite it. Whatever the need, whatever the circumstance, I delight to give to My children. Ask, ask, and then ask some more. You can't wear Me out or overstep your bounds with Me.

"Ask and it will be given to you; seek and you will find; knock and the door will be opened to you. For everyone who asks receives; the one who seeks finds; and to the one who knocks, the door will be opened" (Matthew 7:7–8).

MAY 21
Jesus,

Savior, Redeemer. The Head that should be crowned with glory and honor, crowned with thorns. Rivulets of blood ran from that pierced brow—the brow that should wear heaven's richest adornment. No price was too high for You to pay for my redemption. No possession was more precious to You than my soul. For my sake, You lay down all the riches of glory and took up the Cross instead. Don't let me ever think on my salvation in any way except with utter awe.

"Who, being in very nature God, did not consider equality with God something to be used to his own advantage; rather, he made himself nothing by taking the very nature of a servant, being made

in human likeness. And being found in appearance as a man, he humbled himself by becoming obedient to death—even death on a cross!" (PHILIPPIANS 2:6–8).

MAY 22
Jesus,

I ponder Your stunning act of condescension, Your breathtaking expression of humility. When You were at the pinnacle of the cosmos, King of the universe, none higher or more exalted and adored than You—that's when You emptied Yourself and took on the form of a servant. Came in the form of a peasant woman's illegitimate child, born in a barn, placed in a feeding trough. From the highest in heaven to the lowest on earth. Yet I bristle if someone slights me. I fume if I feel demeaned. I resist obedience that requires I set pride aside. Oh, Savior, chisel the silly pride from my heart and create a heart like Yours.

"The great test of whether the holiness we profess to seek or to attain, is truth and life, will be whether it be manifest in the increasing humility in produces. In the creature, humility is the one thing needed to allow God's holiness to dwell in him and shine through him. . . . The chief mark of counterfeit holiness is its lack of humility. . . . The holiest will be the humblest."

—ANDREW MURRAY, *Humility: The Beauty of Holiness*

MAY 23
Child,

True humility comes from strength. It is not a weakness. Weak people have to puff themselves up to feel important. Pride forces a person to its bidding. Pride requires much vigilant defending and protecting. To protect a sense of importance, a person will miss the great blessings of serving others for no reason other than that the love of Christ compels him to do so. See My Son. See Him strong enough that humility did not lower Him, but exalted Him.

"Jesus knew that the Father had put all things under his power, and that he had come from God and was returning to God; so he got up from the meal, took off his outer clothing, and wrapped a towel around his waist. After that, he poured water into a basin and began to wash his disciples' feet, drying them with the towel that was wrapped around him" (JOHN 13:3–5).

MAY 24
Father,

Apart from Your Spirit, I am helpless to understand Your truth. I need Your Spirit to hand deliver Your truth to my heart through Your word. I love to know that Your word is more than words printed on pages and bound in books. Scripture is Your living voice to me when Your Spirit speaks it to me. Thank You for opening the deep and hidden things in Your word and transforming my life with Your truth.

"Then he opened their minds so they could understand the Scriptures" (LUKE 24:45).

MAY 25
Father,

I'm so easily distracted by shiny new things. On the surface, the cheap imitations the world offers look lovely and inviting. When I find myself spending time, emotions, and money on those things that are only counterfeits and knockoffs of the real treasure You offer, open my eyes. Show me the difference between what is precious and what is worthless. Let me spend my life on the pursuit of real treasure.

"Turn my eyes away from worthless things; preserve my life according to your word" (Psalm 119:37).

MAY 26
Child,

I know you feel discouraged. I know you feel tired and weighted down. Come to Me. I will give you rest. You are trying to carry a burden that you are not built to carry. In this relationship, I carry the load. Hand it over to Me. Right now, give Me the responsibility for that burden. Right now, acknowledge that you believe Me when I tell you that I've got this. Every time the heaviness starts to settle on you again, hand it over. Again and again, until your heart settles into a state of rest.

"He offers his strength for your weakness, his fullness for your emptiness, his power for your inadequacy. He offers you himself and longs to take the weight from your shoulders. You can 'give all your worries and cares to God, for he cares about you' (1 Peter 5:7 [NLT])."
—Jennifer Kennedy Dean, *The One Year Praying the Promises of God*
by Cheri Fuller and Jennifer Kennedy Dean

MAY 27
Child,

I am your refuge, your safe place. I position Myself between you and anything that comes against you. Hide yourself in Me, and let Me take the brunt of the blow for you. Anything headed your way has to get through Me first. Am I strong enough to thwart the impact of life's calamities? Then, hide in Me. Let your heart see this scene: Me—big, powerful, strong; and you—small and hidden behind me; and your calamity—weak and getting weaker trying to get past Me.

"God is our refuge and strength, an ever-present help in trouble. Therefore we will not fear, though the earth give way and the mountains fall into the heart of the sea, though its waters roar and foam and the mountains quake with their surging" (Psalm 46:1–3).

MAY 28
Father,

I feel as though I am caught in a trap. I repeat behaviors I long to escape. I determine and commit to change, and then I find myself right back in the trap. The trap has been cleverly set. I don't see it coming, then find myself in its grip. I feel ashamed and discouraged. Failure again. But then I hear You say that You will deliver me from the snare. You will. Every time, You will pull me free and set my feet on solid ground. I believe that You can accomplish in me what You desire for me. I confess to you that I have come to the end of myself, and look only to You. You will rescue me as many times as it takes until the trap no longer catches me.

"Surely he will save you from the fowler's snare and from the deadly pestilence" (Psalm 91:3).

MAY 29
Child,

Call on Me. I have set up prayer to be the opening from your need to My supply. I'm always ready with every provision you need and all the power necessary for your situation. Everything you need is always flowing in your direction. I call you to prayer so that you would always be aware of My work, and would partner with Me in it through prayer. When you call to Me, I will rescue you is such a way that I am honored and glorified. Call to Me.

"Call on me in the day of trouble; I will deliver you, and you will honor me" (Psalm 50:15).

MAY 30
Jesus,

You are the Vine, and I am Your branch. I embrace that union today. The life circulating in You is flowing right into me. No middleman. Just You into me. I want to be aware of the energizing, purifying flow of You. Produce Your fruit through Me.

"The branch of the vine does not worry, and toil, and rush here to seek for sunshine, and there to find rain. No; it rests in union and communion with the vine; and at the right time, *and in the* right way, *is the* right fruit *found on it. Let us so abide in the Lord Jesus."*
—(James) Hudson Taylor, English missionary to China, 1832–1905,
China's Millions

MAY 31
Child,

Everywhere you set your foot is holy ground. No matter what is occupying you at any given moment, you are standing on holy ground. After all, what made Moses' location holy? Hadn't he passed that way multitudes of times before and the same patch of earth was just ordinary? But on that burning-bush-day, it became holy ground—because of My presence. My presence is a constant with you. I am wherever you are. So, wherever you are is holy ground. Live in an awareness of My presence, and in the background of your thoughts, be always worshipping.

"Take off your sandals, for the place where you are standing is holy ground" (EXODUS 3:5).

June

JUNE 1

Jesus,

I receive fullness from Your fullness. You will never be anything but full. You will never be low on grace or truth. You will always be a fully supplied Fountain that flows into me. A filled cup will soon be empty again, but a cup being filled continually will be always full to overflowing. My fullness comes out of Your never-ending supply. Instead of worrying about whether I'm full, teach me to simply look to Your fullness. Teach me to keep my life open to You and to the grace and truth You pour into me.

"And the Word became flesh, and dwelt among us, and we saw His glory, glory as of the only begotten from the Father, full of grace and truth. . . . For of His fullness we have all received, and grace upon grace" (JOHN 1:14, 16 NASB).

JUNE 2

Child,

Don't forget the ways you see Me work in your life. Gather them up in your heart as great treasures to be guarded and admired and taken out and looked at. Each time you remember My works in your life, take great pleasure in them. We'll build a beautiful collection that will keep growing. Let these treasures build your assurance that what I have done before, I will do again.

"But Mary treasured up all these things and pondered them in her heart" (LUKE 2:19).

JUNE 3

Child,

My energy can work through you. Energy is power in

operation—it propels and compels. My energy works mightily in you. As you submit yourself more and more to Me and to My life in you, you will find that My power is not an abstract idea. Rather, it is a living force that accomplishes My purposes. My life is energetically reaching out to those in your world, and you are the conductive substance through which that power flows. Go out and let My energy touch those you come into contact with today.

"He is the one we proclaim, admonishing and teaching everyone with all wisdom, so that we may present everyone fully mature in Christ. To this end I strenuously contend with all the energy Christ so powerfully works in me" (COLOSSIANS 1:28–29).

JUNE 4
Jesus,

I'm trying to fathom that I am "in Christ." It is mind-boggling that You are in me. But, add to that the fact that I am in You. I don't have to live by earthbound thinking. I am united with You—branch to Vine—and You are seated in heavenly realms. That can be my vantage point. Not, "How does it look from earth?" but instead, "How does it look from heaven?" I can see my life and situation from Your viewpoint. Right now, I am finished telling my story from earth's point of view. That's not the whole picture. I can see it as You see it because I'm with You. I'm not telling my story. I'm telling Your story.

"What does that mean to you and me as we face challenges and opportunities that are too big for us? It means that God 'raised us up from the dead along with Christ and seated us with him in the heavenly realms because we are united with Christ Jesus' (Ephesians 2:6 [NLT]). We are organically connected to Jesus through his Spirit—grafted into the Vine—and we operate from that position. We're already 'with him.' When fear, anxiety, envy, insecurity, or

any of the enemy's lies try to find an opening into your life, stand up, look it in the eye, point to Jesus, and say, 'I'm with him.' Let Jesus take it from there."

—JENNIFER KENNEDY DEAN, *The One Year Praying the Promises of God*
by CHERI FULLER AND JENNIFER KENNEDY DEAN

JUNE 5
Child,

Invisible does not mean imaginary. Nor does it mean insubstantial. Most of the activity of your life is going on in an invisible realm. Really, that's where all the action is. What you do see is responding to the power of what you don't see. Don't live your life trapped in the illusion that what your eyes see tells the whole story. Use the eyes of faith, and look beyond the circumstances of earth. For everything you see in your circumstances, the rest of the story is playing out in the realm you don't see. Count on My unseen activity running the show.

"We fix our eyes not on what is seen, but on what is unseen, since what is seen is temporary, but what is unseen is eternal" (2 CORINTHIANS 4:18).

JUNE 6
Father,

Speak, Lord, Your servant is listening. I want to have the ears of my heart so attuned to Your voice that I will hear it above all the other cacophony that competes for my attention. My own self-interested and self-formulated ideas, the ideas others want me to adopt, the base appeal of the world's illusions, the demand to live for myself—all empty racket. Let me hear Your sweet voice above it all. Your voice is true and steady. My polestar as I navigate this life.

"Just as in prayer it is not we who momentarily catch His attention, but He ours, so when we fail to hear His voice, it is not because He is not speaking so much as that we are not listening. . . . We must recognize that all things are in God and that God is in all things, and we must learn to be very attentive, in order to hear God speaking in His ordinary tone without any special accent."
—CHARLES H. BRENT, *With God in the World: A Series of Papers*

JUNE 7
Child,

When you settle in to My love—really let it take root in you— it will be a driving force in your life. My love will be poured out into your heart (Romans 5:5) and find its expression through you. My love compels to action. It compelled My Son to offer Himself for you. It compelled Me to offer My Son. My love reaches out, seeks out, pursues. Let My love be the impetus to every action.

"For Christ's love compels us" (2 CORINTHIANS 5:14).

JUNE 8
Father,

I'm willing to be poured out like a drink offering for Your sake (Philippians 2:17). It doesn't come naturally to me, but You have so transformed me that I'm ready to hear that call from You. Where do You need to spill me out? Whose life can I enrich by setting my own needs aside? I know that when You ask me to pour out, I am pouring myself out to You, not to another person.

So, let my love for You culminate in acts of selfless service to those You love. Pour me out.

"Christ is the humility of God embodied in human nature; the Eternal Love humbling itself, clothing itself in the garb of meekness and gentleness, to win and serve and save us."

—ANDREW MURRAY, *Humility*

JUNE 9
Child,

You can sleep in peace because I never sleep. I am active on your behalf day and night, with never an interlude or intermission. What's worrying you right now? Tell Me about it, and leave it with Me. Be assured that I knew it before you knew it. I've been working on it since before you had any inkling of a problem. I can do what you can't. All your worrying won't accomplish anything, so just focus on Me instead of on your worry. Fill your mind with Me instead of with your problem.

"Do you not know? Have you not heard? The LORD is the everlasting God, the Creator of the ends of the earth. He will not grow tired or weary, and his understanding no one can fathom" (ISAIAH 40:28).

JUNE 10
Child,

I offer you *perfect* peace. Peace in its fullness. Not the kind of peace the world offers—peace based on circumstances. Fleeting peace. Peace built on a shaky foundation. My peace is perfect. My peace is based on who I am. My peace is based on what I already know about your circumstances. Stay your mind on Me. At first, it will take deciding to change focus from what is wrong to Who is in charge. Do it. As many times as you need to. Then somewhere along the line you'll find your mind stayed on Me. It makes more sense to have Me as the center. My peace is yours right now, and My peace is perfect.

"You keep him in perfect peace whose mind is stayed on You, because he trusts in You" (ISAIAH 26:3 ESV).

JUNE 11
Child,

Repent. Reorient. Change both your thinking and your ways. Turn from the old way of doing and thinking to the new way of doing and thinking. The old way was self-confidence and self-dependence. I have freed you from that desultory way of living—like a dog chasing its tail. Fruitless, never satisfied, worn out living. Leave that behind. Transfer all your confidence from your own ability to My ability.

"Repentance means stepping out of independence back into dependence, and the measure of your repentance will be the measure of your dependence. Every area of your life in which you have not learned to be truly dependent on God is an area of your life in which you have not as yet repented.

"Christ died for us so that He, risen and alive, might now come and dwell within us, so that we might no longer be egocentric, self-oriented, living only for our own interests: 'He died for all, that those who live should live no longer for themselves, but for Him who died for them and rose again' (2 Corinthians 5:15 [NKJV])."

—MAJOR W. IAN THOMAS, *The Indwelling Life of Christ*

JUNE 12
Child,

I will give you what you need when you need it. I don't follow a formula. Even when you have walked with me many years, I will still come to you in surprising ways. You will never, ever be left to figure things out on your own, but I won't necessarily tell you in advance. I'm not your fortune-teller. When you stand in need of wisdom, I will supply it. When you need the right words, I will give them to you. When you need provision, it will be there for you. You can walk out the obedience I've called you to, not knowing in advance how or where or when. Don't concern yourself about supply that you don't need right now. When you need it, it will be there.

"The wise heart will know the proper time and procedure" (ECCLESIASTES 8:5).

JUNE 13
Child,

I make great use of those parts of your walk that take you through darkness. Be assured that your darkness is not dark to Me (Psalm 139:12). You will find treasures in the darkness (Isaiah 45:3), treasures that you will not find in the light. When the way is steep and dark, I lead you as if you were blind and I were leading you along unfamiliar paths. I have you by the hand. I lead you step by careful step. I move the stones out of your path. I steer you around outcroppings. I don't expect you to know the way. I am your way. Beloved, do not be afraid of the dark.

"I will lead the blind by ways they have not known, along unfamiliar paths I will guide them; I will turn the darkness into light before them and make the rough places smooth. These are the things I will do; I will not forsake them" (ISAIAH 42:16).

JUNE 14
Child,

I will tell you things in the dark that you are to speak in the light. You won't stay in the dark. You will learn a certain wisdom in the dark that is for use in the light. The times of darkness are necessary to what you learn about the light. If you've never known the darkness, you won't know the light. Some things are only known by their opposites. You only know up if you know down. You only know in if you know out. You only know light if you know dark. This walk in the darkness is just a short jaunt. Soon you'll be in the light again. Take the lessons of the darkness with you.

"Whatever I tell you in the dark, speak in the light" (Matthew 10:27).

JUNE 15
Child,

When the journey that took you through the darkness gives way to light, you will shine that light to all around you. Something about the work I did in your darkness makes your life shine more intensely. My glory shines on you, and from you. You reflect Me in the light because you walked with Me through the dark. Trust the process. When I lead you into dark places, I have a purpose that the light will bring into view.

"Arise, shine, for your light has come, and the glory of the Lord rises upon you" (Isaiah 60:1).

JUNE 16

Jesus,

My love for You evokes a longing to serve You. I want to do something that will show my love. I want to wash Your feet, or serve You a banquet, or welcome You from a long and tiring journey. I want to serve You! But I hear You say that when I serve my irritating neighbor and get no thanks for the effort, I have served You. When I reach out to a person who is unlovely to me, I have served You. When I lay aside my convenience and preference and meet a need without fanfare, I have served You. If I serve and am admired for it, or if I serve and it wins me an honor, that's one thing. But if I serve and no one even knows, and no one expresses gratitude . . . then I have washed Your feet. Jesus, let me wash Your feet.

"The Son of Man did not come to be served, but to serve" (Matthew 20:28).

JUNE 17

Father,

Its much easier to feel holy when it's just You and me. I get caught up in Your delightful presence, and soak in Your word. Faith flows. Love blooms. I breathe in Your fragrance and revel in Your great love for me. Then I go about my day and it is full of other people—all faulty and unconcerned with my predilections and plans. Not as easy to be holy out here. And yet, out here is just exactly where You call me to holiness—right in the middle of the mess. I surrender to that call. Create such a genuine holiness in me that it holds up out here.

"I will most gladly spend and be expended for your souls"
(2 Corinthians 12:15 NASB).

JUNE 18
Child,

Don't leap to judgment of others. Don't be so quick to put the worst spin on things where others are concerned. Instead of assuming the worst, make a deliberate effort to assume the best. Instead of assigning the worst motives, assume the best motives. I have not given you the job of judging. You don't know what is in anyone's heart. You don't know how you might be if you had exactly the other person's set of life circumstances. When those all around you are calling out judgment, you cry out mercy. If you have to, be the lone voice. Be as merciful toward others as I am merciful toward you.

"Mercy triumphs over judgment" (James 2:13).

JUNE 19
Father,

Feed Your sheep? Your bedraggled, disheveled, always-in-trouble sheep? Your too-fastidious-for-my-liking sheep? Your obnoxious, know-it-all sheep? Wouldn't You like to put some parameters on this command? I hear Your silence. In it I hear Your love for every single sheep, easy-to-love or not. I hear You reminding me that someone fed me when I was rambunctious and misbehaving. Someone feeds me now—and I've got some issues. I remember those along the way who fed me at just the right time in just the right way, in spite of myself. Thank you for Your sheep-feeders. I'll be honored to feed Your sheep.

"Our Lord has many weak children in his family, many dull pupils in his school, many raw soldiers in His army, many lame sheep in His flock. Yet he bears with them all, and casts none away. Happy is that Christian who has learned to deal likewise with his brethren."

—J. C. Ryle, *Expository Thoughts on the Gospel: St. John, volume 3*

JUNE 20
Child,

When your circumstances look as if they will overwhelm you, that's when I make you more than a conqueror. I don't simply lead you through unscathed. I don't simply give you victory over. I do something more than that. Can you imagine something more than that? What's better than conquering? I'll tell you what—more than conquering. Beyond conquering. A superconqueror. Not in spite of, but in the midst of. No matter what happens, because of Me, you win.

"In all these things we are more than conquerors through Him who loved us" (Romans 8:37).

JUNE 21
Father,

I don't want to live poisoned by my past. Mistakes I made, ways I was hurt, times I failed, words that stung. The memories keep returning, and I get caught up in old emotions as if they were present realities. You, Lord, can heal the hurts of my past. I know You don't change the past, but You take the toxins out of old memories. Those who have hurt me did so out of their own woundedness. Your Spirit can replace anger with compassion toward my offender, and set me free from living as a slave to past hurts.

"See, I am doing a new thing! Now it springs up; do you not perceive it? I am making a way in the wilderness and streams in the wasteland." (ISAIAH 42:19).

JUNE 22
Child,

Embrace silence. Plan for times of silence. Sometimes the way I speak is not instant, but rather My voice and My words rise to the surface of your thinking as you cultivate silence, stillness of heart and mind. See how much silence you can fit in today. Those times you typically fill with background noise of some sort so that you won't have to hear silence—see what happens if you let quiet loose. See if it doesn't open your mind to thoughts of Me and your heart to My heart. Just try it and see.

> The Spirit's quiet whisper
> Bids me bow before Your throne
> 'Till my heart's deepest yearnings
> Are the echo of Your own.
> JENNIFER KENNEDY DEAN, © 2000

JUNE 23
Father,

Teach me to be childlike in my response to You. Simple, accepting, trusting, open to the wonder. Like a little child, teach me to just look to You and be completely satisfied that You know what I don't know, that You have what I don't have, that You are caring for my best interests. Like a child depending on her parents without puzzling it out, teach me to walk in freedom from worry and care because You are my Daddy and that's all I need to know.

"Let the little children come to me, and do not hinder them, for the kingdom of God belongs to such as these" (MATTHEW 19:14).

JUNE 24
Father,

So shape my heart and regulate my life that I am a genuine and accurate expression of Your Son in the world. Whatever it takes to remove distortions of who He is, do that deep work in me. Let me be so full of Your Spirit and so flooded with the life of Your Son that anything other than the full expression of Him is flushed out with the tide of His presence.

"And we know that in all things God works for the good of those who love him, who have been called according to his purpose. For those God foreknew he also predestined to be conformed to the image of his Son, that he might be the firstborn among many brothers and sisters" (ROMANS 8:28–29).

JUNE 25
Child,

I am Love. Love is My very makeup. Everything I do comes from love. Even discipline and correction, even difficult times of shaping and restoring—all from love. I'm never trying to prove a point or see how far I can push you. Only love. All love all the time. Trust that I have no plan for you that is not conceived and born in love. I seek and plan for only your good and benefit. Trust My love for you.

"But when the kindness and love of God our Savior appeared, he saved us, not because of righteous things we had done, but because of his mercy" (TITUS 3:4–5).

JUNE 26
Child,

When I call you to love, I have not called you to an emotion, but to a decision. Walk in love. Act in love. Respond in love. Do love.

"Love is the first and the chief among the streams of living water that are to flow from us.

"Love is the fulfilling of the law. It 'worketh no ill to his neighbour' (Romans 13:10 [KJV]). It 'seeketh not her own' (1 Corinthians 13:5). 'It causes us to lay down our lives for the brethren' [sic] (1 John 3:16). Our hearts become ever larger and larger."

—ANDREW MURRAY, *Experiencing the Holy Spirit*

JUNE 27
Child,

My love is poured into your heart through My Spirit (Romans 5:5). It is always pouring from My heart to yours. You can't use it up because it is a never-ending stream pouring and pouring and pouring into you. The more you pour out, the more I pour in. Do you want to live in a mighty flow of love? Then give love away. Look for opportunities.

"He, who is crucified love, has filled our heart completely with Himself. We are rooted in love. In accordance with the nature of the root, God produces the fruit-love. Souls, listen to the Word: 'God is love.' He has provided everything that you may know love fully. It is with this aim that Christ desires to have your whole heart. Begin to pray that the Father would strengthen us with might by the Spirit, and that we may know the love of Christ."

—ANDREW MURRAY, *Experiencing the Holy Spirit*

JUNE 28
Child,

Prove love genuine. Respond in love when love is the unexpected response. Surprise others with My love. When loving forgiveness stands where anger and resentment were expected, what could explain it? When gentleness emerges when harshness was anticipated, what could explain it? When you turn the other cheek when backlash was assumed, what can explain it? Act and live in love not your own. Express My love and there will be no explanation except Christ in you.

"Do everything in love" (1 CORINTHIANS 16:14).

JUNE 29
Child,

Everything I have ever done or will ever do is designed to reveal Myself to the chosen objects of My love. I am present and available and here for you. I created the earth to be a visible manifestation of My invisible qualities (Romans 1:20). When I created human beings, I created them to be My image in the world (Genesis 1:26). When I sent My Son, it was to reveal My nature and My infinite love (John 1:14, 18). I make Myself known. You feel that I am obscuring Myself in your present situation. You feel that you can't find Me. But, beloved child, I am here. I am revealing Myself. Relax, rest. You will see Me. You are looking for Me in a prescribed form, a way I've revealed Myself to you before. But I'm revealing Myself in a new way. Stop striving. I'm in charge of the revealing.

"The one who loves me will be loved by my Father, and I too will love them and show myself to them" (JOHN 14:21).

JUNE 30
Child,

My highest call is to the lowest duty. When I call you to obedience that no one will see or know about, or that will not advance you or your reputation, and that will have no payoff for you other than My glory—that is obedience that honors and thrills Me most. It will require an infusion of My love and My motivations because it is not possible in the power of your flesh. Consider it an honor when I call you to such an action.

"Now that I, your Lord and Teacher, have washed your feet, you also should wash one another's feet. I have set you an example that you should do as I have done for you. Very truly I tell you, no servant is greater than his master, nor is a messenger greater than the one who sent him. Now that you know these things, you will be blessed if you do them" (JOHN 13:14–17).

July

JULY 1
Child,

Everything serves Me. All circumstances, all situations, even all people are serving My purposes. Don't be distressed or dismayed. Nothing has slipped by Me. Nothing has escaped My notice. Leave it all to Me.

"The LORD has made everything for its own purpose, Even the wicked for the day of evil" (PROVERBS 16:4).

JULY 2
Child,

I want you to be in My inner circle. I long for you to know the mysteries that I only reveal to My beloved children. I want you to know My depths so that you can have perfect, uninterrupted confidence in Me. I want you to live in peace. You are secure in Me. I have wonderful, beautiful provision for you. Everything you need is set aside and marked with your name. Would you let it into your life? Would you listen to My voice? Would you receive the deep truth that I want you to understand? Linger with Me and much of what I want to reveal will come by osmosis . . . it will just seep into your thoughts and understanding through prolonged contact with Me.

"What no eye has seen, what no ear has heard, and what no human mind has conceived—the things God has prepared for those who love him—these are the things God has revealed to us by his Spirit" (1 CORINTHIANS 2:9–10).

JULY 3
Child,

What worries you? Tell Me about it. Then take time to listen to Me and let Me speak My promises to you. I will give you peace and assurance. What are you lacking? Ask Me for it. Listen to Me and I will guide you into My provision. Let Me teach you how to use the senses of your spirit so that you can know Me the way I long for you to know Me.

"Open your mouth wide and I will fill it" (PSALM 81:10).

JULY 4
Child,

I want to confide in you—tell you My secrets. I want you to know Me as an intimate friend. We don't just chitchat or small talk. We get to the heart of the matter. Because you are privy to My confidences, it creates an intimacy between us that carries into our whole relationship, every minute, every day. Just a look can pass between us and we know. Live in My presence and let Me communicate My heart to you. Treasure what I share with you and let it transform you.

"The LORD confides in those who fear him; he makes his covenant known to them" (PSALM 25:14).

JULY 5
Father,

I want to know You. I don't want anything more than I want to know the secrets of Your kingdom. I trust You completely with every need and every desire. I give them to You—they are Yours. I no longer own any need or any desire because I am turning them over to you. From now on, when I feel needs and desires, I will know that I am feeling Your needs and desires. I know that in meeting my needs and fulfilling my deepest desires and longings, You are putting Your will on the earth. I trust You. You are not working against me, but for me.

"For the LORD *. . . takes the upright into his confidence"* (PROVERBS 3:32).

JULY 6
Father,

Let me understand Your ways. Fill me with the knowledge of Your will. Forgive me for focusing my attention on the circumstances of this earth, opening the door to anxiety. Forgive me for thinking of Your Glory in terms too small and limited. Expand my vision until it matches Yours.

"Now to him who is able to do immeasurably more than all we ask or imagine, according to his power that is at work within us, to him be glory in the church and in Christ Jesus throughout all generations, for ever and ever!" (EPHESIANS 3:20–21).

JULY 7
Child,

I have done such transforming work in you that I have to call it a heart transplant. I describe the old heart as a "heart of stone." It is lifeless. It cannot receive or dispense the flow of blood. It is hardened and impenetrable. It cannot be shaped and molded. In contrast, the new heart I have given is a "heart of flesh." It pulses. It takes in and pumps out life. The old heart is to the new heart as stone is to flesh. They are not even in the same category. The two are entirely different entities. One is dead and eroding, the other is alive and growing stronger day by day.

"I will give you a new heart and put a new spirit in you; I will remove from you your heart of stone and give you a heart of flesh. And I will put my Spirit in you and move you to follow my decrees and be careful to keep my laws" (EZEKIEL 36:26–27).

JULY 8
Child,

When a patient receives a heart transplant, what is the patient's part in the operation? Is he to give the surgeon direction? Is the surgeon looking to him for help, expecting him to be involved in the surgical procedure? Surely not. If the patient were to try to help the surgeon perform the surgery, he would only limit the surgeon and complicate the procedure. The patient is to yield himself to the work of the surgeon. The patient doesn't have to understand the intricacies of the procedure; he simply has to put himself into the surgeon's hands. Your willingness to yield is all I need. Hand yourself over. I can take if from there.

"It is God who works in you to will and to act in order to fulfill his good purpose" (PHILIPPIANS 2:13).

JULY 9
Child,

Trust Me to move you to do My will. Move ahead, step-by-step, allowing Me to express My will through your yielded will. What one step do you need to take to move forward on your best understanding of My will? It will probably be something small and simple. Step-by-step, I will open and close doors, bring you into contact with the right people, lead you to the needed information. At each step, remain yielded. You cannot anticipate the turns in the road. The road may have a different destination than you anticipated when you took the first step, but I am leading you in My way. What is the step in front of you? Do that.

"I will instruct you and teach you in the way you should go; I will counsel you with my loving eye on you" (PSALM 32:8).

JULY 10
Child,

You are the child of My heart. I created you because I find pleasure in you. You exist because I will you to exist. I want you to find all the joy, meaning, and purpose I have always meant for you to have. Everything I have for you is in My Son. As My life flows through Him and His life flows through you—I am directing you in the path of joy. Yield to Me so that I can possess every part of you and set you free to live in My fullness. I'm the One moving you to do My will. Wherever you're letting Me, I'm living through you. I'm the One changing you. I'm the one motivating you. I want to show you the places in you that you do not want to make available to Me—the places inside you that you've fenced off as your own. I want to show you because, right there, I long to pour out My power. In maintaining ownership, you are settling for much less than I have planned. Hand me the title deed, and I will tear down the fences. I will move in. I will take possession. I will . . . I will . . . I will.

"May not a single moment of my life be spent outside the light, love, and joy of God's presence. And not a moment without the entire surrender of myself as a vessel for Him to fill full of His Spirit and His love."

—ANDREW MURRAY

JULY 11

Father,

I realize that anything about me that even slightly resembles You is the result of Your work. I have done nothing and can never do anything to make myself like You. I can't change myself anymore than stone can change itself into flesh—anymore than a leopard can change its spots. I want You to fill me, saturate me, drench me from the inside out. Take over every corner of me. Now that I have tasted Your life, I can never be satisfied with anything else. Move me to do Your will and be careful to keep Your laws. There are areas of my life that I sense You asking for today. I am inviting You to move in and possess the areas I hear You speaking to me about.

"Taste and see that the LORD is good" (PSALM 34:8).

JULY 12

Father,

You know the longing in me that is so deep I can't find the words to express it. You created that longing. I am like a parched land where there is no water. I can't soak up enough of You. I want to know You intimately. "Guide me in your truth and teach me" (Psalm 25:5). "I rejoice in your promise like one who finds great spoil" (Psalm 119:162). "The law from your mouth is more precious to me than thousands of pieces of silver and gold" (Psalm 119:72). Let my mind and understanding be the tablet on which You write. I offer myself to You. Let me be the vehicle through which You do Your work in my world. Let Your words come from my mouth. Father, as I meditate on Your Word day and night, don't let Your words depart out of my mouth. Keep my mouth filled with Your words. I don't want to fill my mouth with any other words that would crowd Your words out.

"This book of the law shall not depart from your mouth, but you shall meditate on it day and night, so that you may be careful to do according to all that is written in it; for then you will make your way prosperous, and then you will have success" (Joshua 1:8 NASB).

JULY 13
Child,

You are longing to hear Me speak, and I am longing to speak. Don't let the fear of hearing Me incorrectly, or mistaking My voice for your imagination, stop you. Don't worry about your ability to hear. Trust My ability to speak. I'm initiating this interchange. We'll start out slowly while you learn the language of Spirit. I'll speak in your vocabulary. One step at a time. Here—take hold of My hand. Sit at My feet. Leave it all to Me. I will separate out My voice from your imagination.

"My sheep listen to my voice; I know them, and they follow me" (John 10:27).

JULY 14
Child,

Your life has a purpose. I created you and designed you exactly how I want you. Everything about you is related to your purpose and destiny, so your destiny fits you exactly. A strong sense of purpose produces joy. Even the hard times and the confusing circumstances and the seeming setbacks will be fused into an understanding of destiny. The person who lives with a focused purpose will see life as something like a jigsaw puzzle, each piece fitting into a pattern to produce the whole. If you were to look at a single piece of a jigsaw puzzle, it would seem meaningless and random. Yet when you place it in its assigned position, it becomes an integral part of the picture. When one piece of the puzzle is missing, the picture is not whole. When you look at the circumstances of your life as if each could stand alone, and as if each situation should make sense on its own, you will never see the big picture. Only when you view each happening as a significant piece of a whole will you begin to see life as integrated and meaningful. As I work in your life, I am keeping My eye on the big picture. I am directing you in the way you should go.

"In the infinite wisdom of the Lord of all the earth, each event falls with exact precision into its proper place in the unfolding of His divine plan. Nothing, however small, however strange, occurs without His ordering, or without its particular fitness for its place in the working out of His purpose; and the end of all shall be the manifestation of His glory, and the accumulation of His praise."

—B. B. Warfield

JULY 15
Child,

I formed you exactly how I needed you to be, to fulfill My purpose for you. I have already marked out a path for you to follow. Along that path you will find your longings fulfilled; you will find your needs met. Along that path, marked out for no one except you, you will find yourself in Me. I have placed all of your provisions along your path. You will not find them along anyone else's path. They are waiting for you on the path marked with your name. As you walk your path, you will encounter the good deeds I have assigned you to do. I assigned them before you existed. Don't try to do anyone else's deeds. They are not assigned for you. You have to fix your eyes on Me and keep your ears open toward Me so that I can lead you step by step along your path.

Every time you come to a decision, I'll be there saying, "This is the way. Walk in it." I want you to be completely abandoned to Me. I want to have access to all of you. I want your fixed attention at all times. Follow Me. I will fill you with joy.

"Given a man full of faith, you will have a man tenacious in purpose, absorbed in one grand object, simple in his motives, in whom selfishness has been driven out by the power of a mightier love, and indolence stirred into unwearied energy."

—ALEXANDER MACLAREN, *Exposition of Holy Scripture: St. Matthew Chaps. IX to XXVIII*

JULY 16
Father,

You have filled my life with such a deep sense of purpose. I can't imagine living without meaning. You need me. I know that You only need me because You have chosen to need me, but still You need me to fulfill my purpose so that You can fulfill Your purpose. Every day of my life is an adventure as I walk deeper into Your purpose for me. Remember when I first sensed a personal destiny? Remember how cautiously I started down my path? The way seemed so dark and unknowable, but You kept encouraging me to take baby steps. Sometimes I stumbled over obstacles I didn't see. Sometimes I skinned a knee. But You always picked me up and moved me on. The farther I traveled, the more clear the path became. More often than not, I now see the obstacles before I trip over them. The journey is shaping me. I am becoming stronger and bolder as I travel. I still have a long way to go, but now sometimes I can even pick up the pace for a while. I love the path You have chosen for me!

"More men fail through lack of purpose than lack of talent."

—BILLY SUNDAY

JULY 17
Father,

Single-minded concentration, clear focus, directed vision, a runner racing for the finish line, distractions blocked out, hard-won goal in view: this is the faith journey. When it hit me that knowing Jesus—really knowing Him, not just being acquainted—*knowing* Jesus is of surpassing worth, those goals I once cherished shriveled up and dropped off like a dry leaf in winter. It is of more value than anything in life. Worth more by leaps and bounds than any other goal. *Surpassing* worth. I have discovered something of surpassing worth. I'm pressing in to that goal.

"I press on to take hold of that for which Christ Jesus took hold of me. . . . Forgetting what is behind and straining toward what is ahead, press on toward the goal to win the prize for which God has called me heavenward in Christ Jesus" (PHILIPPIANS 3:12–14).

JULY 18
Child,

Take hold of that for which Christ Jesus took hold of you. My intent for you is to know Him and to live by faith in Him, putting no faith in your own efforts at goodness. Have you taken hold of that for which Christ Jesus took hold of you? From your earthbound perspective, it seems that you are pursuing Him. It feels to you as though you crave relationship with Him, and so put your heart into developing the intimacy that you are convinced is possible. But really, He has sought you out. You long for Him because He longs for you. You love Him because He first loved you. You press on toward Him because He is drawing you. What feels like initiative is really a response. Always the Word is: "Here

I am! I stand at the door and knock. If anyone hears my voice and opens the door, I will come in and eat with that person and he with me" (Revelation 3:20). You yearn for what He is offering because His invitation has awakened your desire. You are the object of His love. He is devoted to you. Surrender to His pursuit.

"Difficulties and obstacles are God's challenges to faith. When hindrances confront us in the path of duty, we are to recognize them as vessels for faith to fill with the fullness and all-sufficiency of Jesus."

—A. B. Simpson

JULY 19
Child,

"Forgetting what is behind and straining toward what is ahead, I press on." Look carefully at what the Spirit is teaching you. The way to move forward is to be disentangled from your past. Forget what is behind. Neglect the past. Don't nourish the past; don't give any attention to your past, no matter how loudly it demands it. Neglect your past and let it die of malnourishment. If you want to seize with both hands the purpose for which Jesus has seized you, you have to leave behind every piece of your past—both its failures and its successes. You have flesh-born patterns of behavior that you have relied on to attract love and feel valued. Is this harder for you than leaving behind past failures and sins? Stop using your tried-and-true approval-getting methods, and have faith only in Him, You don't have to perform and dazzle and please everyone to be loved. You are so loved, just as you are.

"Men have presented their plans and philosophies for the remedying of earth's ills, but Jesus stands alone in presenting not a system, but His own personality as capable of supplying the needs of the soul."

—A. C. Dixon

JULY 20

Child,

I call you to a reckless obedience. Obedience without caution, and heedless of danger. The reason you can obey Me recklessly is because I am careful over you. You can trust Me with the consequences of My call. Once you learn to trust My wisdom implicitly, My commands no longer have the ring of foolishness to them. Reckless obedience to My voice is what I'm looking for. When I find a person of uncompromising obedience, who doesn't hesitate for fear of the consequences, I pour out My power in that one. The one who has learned that "whoever obeys his command will come to no harm" (Ecclesiastes 8:5), can leave the consequences in My hands and obey fearlessly. I don't give foolish commands. They only seem foolish when evaluated with human wisdom. I deal with you wisely, always careful over you and mindful of your humanity. I don't require anything I am not willing to supply.

"I, the LORD have called you in righteousness; I will take hold of your hand" (ISAIAH 42:6).

JULY 21

Child,

As you obey My commands, all you have to do is rely fully on Me. Your inability does not matter. I don't shrink the size of My power to fit within your abilities; I expand your abilities to accommodate the size of My power. My power is most visible in your weakness. Rejoice in your weaknesses—embrace them, celebrate them. They are the perfect background against which I can display My power. Your weaknesses will compliment My power perfectly. "The way of the LORD is a refuge for the blameless" (Proverbs 10:29). When you are following My command, you are safe and protected. My way, the way I am directing you, is a refuge. But refusing to risk all on My call is not safe. It is dangerous. In choosing to ignore My call, you are choosing to step outside of the flow of My power. I am not withdrawing from you, but you are withdrawing from Me. By disobedience, you have willfully moved yourself out of My stream of blessing. I love you too much to leave you there. I will do whatever is necessary to pull you back. Until you surrender to My call, you will have to actively resist My urging. It will wear you down. It's easier and it's safer to obey Me when I call. My way is your refuge.

"You have laid down precepts that are to be fully obeyed. Oh, that my ways were steadfast in obeying your decrees! Then I would not be put to shame when I consider all your commands" (PSALM 119:4–6).

JULY 22
Child,

I will work patiently and gently with you as you struggle to the point of obedience when My call looks risky or difficult. Jesus had to struggle through His human fears to reach the point of calm and serenity that He displayed during His trial and humiliation. When you are in the struggle, you have not removed yourself from the flow of My power. Only when you refuse have you moved out of the stream. Time and experience will teach you this: sometimes you will enter into obedience saying, "Do I *have* to?" But in the center of obedience you will always find yourself saying, "Do I *get* to?" Every time you struggle through to obedience, you'll say, "Thank you, Father, for getting me here. Imagine what I'd have missed out on if I had given in to fear and refused Your Voice." Obedience comes more easily as you build a history with Me and learn that My call is always for your advancement. When you are obeying My command, you will come to no harm. You will know what you need to know when you need to know it.

"There's some task which the God of all the universe, the great Creator, your redeemer in Jesus Christ has for you to do, and which will remain undone and incomplete until by faith and obedience you step into the will of God."

—ALAN REDPATH

JULY 23
Child,

My plan for you is not to limit, but to expand. "He reached down from on high and took hold of me; . . . He brought me out into a spacious place" (Psalm 18:16, 19). "You broaden the path beneath me, so that my ankles do not turn" (Psalm 18:36). Set your heart on things above. Set your heart on the realities that cannot be seen with earthly eyes. Set your heart on the things that Jesus is dispensing from His seat at My right hand. Set your heart on what Jesus is doing in every circumstance. Refuse the distractions. Turn away from the shadow; embrace the substance. You cannot know the truth of a matter until you have taken into account the things above.

Don't focus your eyes on what you can see—the circumstances of earth. Instead, focus your eyes on the facts and realities of the spiritual realm—My sovereignty, the authority of Jesus, the power of the Spirit. Let your spiritual senses mature until you have spiritual depth perception and can experience life in the spacious place into which I am calling you.

"We must learn to live on the heaven side and look at things from above. How it overcomes sin, deifies [sic] Satan, resolves perplexities, lifts us above trials, separates us from the world and conquers the fear of death to contemplate all things as God sees them."

—A. B. SIMPSON, *Days of Heaven Upon Earth: A Year Book of Scripture Texts and Living Truths*

JULY 24
Child,

I am in the details. I am engineering even the smallest detail in order to establish My divine purpose in every situation. Happenings that seem random, choices and decisions that seem spontaneous and uncalculated, paths that cross in a seemingly serendipitous way—all are being put in order by My deliberate hand. "The lot is cast into the lap, but its every decision is from the LORD" (Proverbs 16:33). Does anything seem more random than the casting of a lot? Yet even that which seems unplanned or uncontrolled—a lot cast into the lap—is really being ordered by Me.

"In the infinite wisdom of the Lord of all the earth, each event falls with exact precision into its proper place in the unfolding of His eternal plan; nothing, however small, however strange, occurs without His ordering, or without its peculiar fitness for its place in the working out of His purpose; and the end of all shall be the manifestation of His glory, and the accumulation of His praise."

—B. B. WARFIELD

JULY 25
Child,

When you know My ways and recognize the underlying consistency in all My doings, you will learn to see the divine will in the center of everything. It is My way to manage the details, to act according to an eternal plan. "I will exalt you and praise your name, for in perfect faithfulness you have done wonderful things, things planned long ago" (Isaiah 25:1). Whatever is happening in your life right now, even though it may seem out of control, even though it may seem as if circumstances are taking on a momentum of their own, I am acting according to a plan that has been in place since the beginning of time. It may look as if the lot has been randomly cast in your lap, but remember every decision is from Me. "The lot is cast into the lap, but its every decision is from the Lord" (Proverbs 16:33).

"A providence is shaping our ends; a plan is developing in our lives; a supremely wise and loving Being is making all things work together for good."

—F. B. Meyer, *Paul: A Servant of Jesus Christ*

JULY 26
Child,

My kingdom works on a principle that I'll call "the principle of progressive revelation." Nothing springs forth full-grown. Everything in the material creation and everything in the spiritual realm is progressively revealed. It requires both faith and patience to receive the promises. "We do not want you to become lazy, but to imitate those who through faith and patience inherit what has been promised . . . And so after waiting patiently, Abraham received what was promised" (Hebrews 6:12, 15). The promises that are your inheritance—your certain possession—will not come into your life full-grown. I promised Abraham: "I will surely bless you and give you many descendants" (Hebrews 6:14). Yet this promise was progressively unfolded. I did not make the promise and fulfill the promise on the same day. A long period of time elapsed between the promise and its fulfillment. Abraham had to exercise faith and patience before the fulfillment of the promise entered his experience. Don't be either surprised or discouraged that the promises I have made you seem long in coming. Have faith and patience.

"If the Lord Jehovah makes us wait, let us do so with our whole hearts;

for blessed are all they that wait for Him. He is worth waiting for. The waiting itself is beneficial to us: it tries faith, exercises patience, trains submission, and endears the blessing when it comes. The Lord's people have always been a waiting people."

—CHARLES SPURGEON, *The Treasury of David, vol. VII, Psalm CXXV to CL*

JULY 27
Child,

This time of unobservable work, this time during which the seed is germinating, is a time of activity and a time in which My power is operating mightily. You will only know this work by faith because faith is what connects your earthly mind to spiritual reality. Don't mistake the appearance of inactivity for delay. I am not delaying; I am working in the invisible realm. What is happening in the invisible realm is going to show up in the visible realm. First the stalk, then the head, then the full kernel in the head.

"This is what the kingdom of God is like. A man scatters seed on the ground. Night and day, whether he sleeps or gets up, the seed sprouts and grows, though he does not know how. All by itself the soil produces grain—first the stalk, then the head, then the full kernel in the head. As soon as the grain is ripe, he puts the sickle to it, because the harvest has come" (MARK 4:26–29).

JULY 28
Child,

Is an obstacle in your way? Nothing is an obstacle to Me. Every roadblock will turn out to be to your advantage. I have uses for obstacles. Sometimes I allow an obstacle to keep you from taking an action before the timing is right. If an obstacle can stand, it is because I have ordained it to stand for a time. Sometimes I use obstacles to redirect you. I use obstacles to mature your faith and teach you how to look to Me and not to obstacles in your way. Mountains in the road are My tools and are useful to Me in guiding you.

"I will turn all my mountains into roads, and my highways will be raised up" (ISAIAH 49:11).

JULY 29
Child,

My presence leaves its mark on you. You can't be in My presence and not be changed by the experience. When I used to talk to Moses face to face like a man talks to his friend, the skin on Moses' face radiated the encounter. I was outside Moses. His face's radiance faded. I'm inside You. I'm closer than I was to Moses. My presence doesn't shine off your skin. It shines from your heart. You life becomes radiant with Me. The changes in you do not fade, but get stronger and brighter. Don't veil My presence in your life. Let Me shine. Be transparent and real to those around you and they will see Me.

"Now the Lord is the Spirit, and where the Spirit of the Lord is, there is freedom. And we all, who with unveiled faces contemplate the Lord's glory, are being transformed into his image with ever-increasing glory, which comes from the Lord, who is the Spirit" (2 CORINTHIANS 3:17–18).

JULY 30
Father,

How tenderly You call my name, offering eternity, drawing me ever deeper into Your great heart. Like a magnet, Your irresistible pull is unrelenting. I surrender to Your gentle wooing, at last to find that You are my heart's cry.

"Show me your face, let me hear your voice; for your voice is sweet, and your face is lovely" (Song of Songs 2:14).

JULY 31
Father,
  "Draw near, My child," is Your sweet call. My heart yearns to enter into Your beckoning Light. The services I have performed for You, the rituals to ensure Your favor, have left me empty. I can't seem to get beyond the veil, where the alluring brightness of Your glory shines. Then I hear You say, "Rest, abide. These are the mysteries. Your works won't show the way. Look to My Son. He is the Open Door into My presence. Lose yourself in Him to find your way to Me."

"See, I have placed before you an open door that no one can shut" (Revelation 3:8).

August

AUGUST 1
Child,

Let Me do My work in you. Let Me free you from yourself. Let Me show you that your truest self, your highest self, is yet to be. Not in anger will I refine you, but in love greater than you can conceive. Come to Me in the full assurance of faith. Rest here. Rest from all your futile attempts at purity. Let Me display My strength through your weakness. Let Me do what you cannot.

"I will give them a heart to know me, that I am the Lord"
(Jeremiah 24:7).

AUGUST 2
Child,

Follow Me. Live My life in your world. Express My love. Speak My words. You are My chosen instrument. You are living proof that I Am.

"Today if you hear His voice, do not harden your hearts"
(Hebrews 4:7).

AUGUST 3
Father,

I feel that I am on the fringes of Your kingdom. I have touched the hem of Your garment but have not looked into Your face. I believe in You, but I sense no power in prayer. There is a gnawing hunger in my soul. Then I hear You say, "My child, the work I will do is eternal. I do not respond to your demands. I respond to your heart's cry. I will satisfy that hunger in your soul. I will fill your emptiness. Feast at My table."

"I am the bread of life. He who comes to me will never go hungry" (JOHN 6:35).

AUGUST 4
Father,

Weed out bitterness. Let praise take root and flourish. Cultivate my life so that it will display Your beauty. Make my life like a watered garden, lush with the Spirit's fruit.

"You will be like a well-watered garden" (ISAIAH 58:11).

AUGUST 5
Child,

Think My thoughts. Empty yourself, and become a servant. Bear on your heart the world's needs. Let go of your desires for toys and short-term delights. Embrace eternity; store up everlasting treasure. Enter into My joy.

"Have the same mindset as Christ Jesus: . . . he made Himself nothing by taking the very nature of a servant. . . . Therefore God exalted Him to the highest place" (PHILIPPIANS 2:5, 7, 9).

AUGUST 6
Father,

Thank You for my needs because they lead me to Your supply. Glorify Yourself through my needs. Most of all, Father, use my needs to establish Your kingdom and Your righteousness.

"And my God will meet all your needs according to his glorious riches in Christ Jesus" (Philippians 4:19).

AUGUST 7
Father,

Push back the noise. Your secrets come wrapped in silence.

"He says, 'Be still, and know that I am God; I will be exalted among the nations, I will be exalted in the earth'" (Psalm 46:10).

AUGUST 8
Father,

How easily I trade away my eternal birthright for momentary ease. I want quick fixes and easy answers. I will give You words of love, but not my time. The disquiet in my soul never ends. Then I hear You: "Everything you're searching for is waiting here, in Me."

"Come to me . . . I will give you rest" (Matthew 11:28).

AUGUST 9
Father,

When I step away from the noise of my life and let silence seep into my soul, I find that I am desperate for You. When all life's embellishments that divert my attention, and all the commotion that distracts me from Your whisper is quieted, I find in myself such a desire for Your face that I fall to my knees in the sanctuary of my own soul. There is no other logical response. I realize that all the noise and the distractions are the tools my enemy uses to keep me from addressing my vital need to be fully connected in heart to You.

"You, God, are my God, earnestly I seek you; I thirst for you, my whole being longs for you, in a dry and parched land where there is no water" (PSALM 63:1).

AUGUST 10
Father,

In my worship and adoration of You, joy settles in. I was created to revere and glorify You, and when I walk in worship, I feel at home. When thoughts of You are front and center, all of life looks different. Fear can't find a foothold. Worry can't get purchase. Resentment dissipates. Anger finds no place to land. When I'm all taken up with You, You allow no interlopers. Worship takes the enemy's best weapons out of rotation.

"Blessed are those who have learned to acclaim you, who walk in the light of your presence, LORD. They rejoice in your name all day long; they celebrate your righteousness. For you are their glory and strength" (PSALM 89:15–17).

AUGUST 11
Child,

End your anxious search, Beloved. To find My presence, look no further than your own heart. I have erected My tabernacle, My dwelling place, in your spirit. You are always in My presence. My presence is My gift to you. Learn to realize and enjoy My presence. I *am* everything you need, and I *am* in you.

"You will fill me with joy in your presence, with eternal pleasures at your right hand" (PSALM 16:11).

AUGUST 12
Child,

The longing you feel to know Me intimately, to live in My presence, is but the shadow cast by My longing for your presence. How intensely I yearn over you. Relax and let Me draw you into My strong arms.

"It is important now that you cease from self-action and self-exerting in attempting to experience His presence. God Himself can act alone."
—MADAME GUYON, *Experiencing God Through Prayer*

AUGUST 13
Child,

I am drawing you to Myself—away from the noise and bustle of the world into the wilderness where I can speak tenderly to you. "Therefore I am now going to allure her; I will lead her into the wilderness and speak tenderly to her" (Hosea 2:14). Go with Me there. Listen for My whisper. I want to give you fresh manna.

"Jesus has pulled you into His inner circle, those to whom He will impart His secrets. Listen. 'I have called you friends, for everything that I learned from my Father I have made known to you' (John 15:15). A person who is following a doctrine need not listen. There is nothing new to know. The one who is following Christ must be continually listening. Spoken prayer is your response to what you have heard."

—JENNIFER KENNEDY DEAN, *Heart's Cry*

AUGUST 14

Father, as I soak myself in Your presence, saturate me with Yourself. Seep into my spirit pores until I am filled with You. Let me breathe in Your love for me, and breathe it out again toward You. You are my treasure, and my heart knows no other home.

"We must know before we can love. In order to know God, we must often think of Him; and when we come to love Him, we shall also think of Him often, for our heart will be with our treasure."
—BROTHER LAWRENCE, *The Practice of the Presence of God*

AUGUST 15
Father,

My Heart's Desire, empty me of anything that is cluttering my life and keeping You from having free access. Scrub away the shards of broken bric-a-brac. Those things that once distracted me from You have revealed themselves, finally, to be fragile and worthless. The floors of my heart are strewn with their wreckage. Clean out Your dwelling place and fill it with Your glory.

"I know that for the right practice of [the presence of God] the heart must be empty of all other things, because God will possess the heart alone; and as He cannot possess it alone without emptying it of all besides, no neither can He act there, and do in it what He pleases, unless it be left vacant to Him."
—BROTHER LAWRENCE, *The Practice of the Presence of God*

AUGUST 16

Father, fill my heart so completely that no room is left for anything else. Take up all the space. Hear my heart's cry: "Only You. Only You."

"Our hearts belong to Him alone and He can plant them in His divine desires and make them ours. Enthroned in our lives, He can channel His good plans into the world through our prayers. By allowing our lives to be absorbed in His, we can bit by bit be freed of our shortsighted desires and participate in eternity."

—Jennifer Kennedy Dean, *Live a Praying Life*

AUGUST 17

Father,

The longer I remain quietly in Your presence, the freer I become. I find that I am no longer weighed down with anxieties. I am no longer bound and restricted by the opinions of others. My feet are no longer immersed in the world's sludge. You have given me feet like the feet of deer. You enable me to stand on the heights.

> Behold, what Love is this
> That reaches out for me
> And lifts me from the miry clay
> To set my spirit free?

—Jennifer Kennedy Dean ©2000

AUGUST 18

Father,

Your presence is in me. When I leave my solitude to enter into the world, Your presence goes with me. Teach me to carry the peace and freedom I find in times alone with You in the hustle and bustle of life. Keep me aware of Your presence continually.

"What is here urged are internal practices and habits of the mind. What is here urged are secret habits of unceasing orientation of the deeps of our being about the Inward Light, ways of conducting our inward life so that we are perpetually bowed in worship, while we are also very busy in the world of daily affairs. What is here urged are inward practices of the mind at deepest levels, letting it swing like the needle, to the polestar of the soul."

—Thomas R. Kelly, *A Testament of Devotion*

AUGUST 19

Jesus,

When You moved out of eternity into time, when You left divine order for human chaos; when You traded Your throne for a manger—You had no other reason than love for me.

Oh, Lord Jesus, dwell in me in all Your fullness.
It was for me
He took on the time and space constraints of earth
Let a veil of flesh conceal His worth
Set redemption's plan in motion with His birth
It was for me.
It was for me
He gave up His flesh—an offering for my sin
Let God's wrath toward me be spent on Him
Poured out His life so my life could begin
It was for me.
It was for me

He threw off the time and space constraints of earth
Shed His veil of flesh, revealed His worth
Opened up for me the way to the Spirit birth
It was for me.
—Jennifer Kennedy Dean © 2008

AUGUST 20

Jesus,

Thank You for being made into the image of man so that I could be remade in the image of You.

"I praise and glorify Thee, O Eternal Wisdom of the Father, for the amazing descent of Thy unattainable Majesty into the common prison-house of our mortal nature."

—Thomas à Kempis, *Meditations on the Life of Christ*

AUGUST 21

Child,

For you I gave My Son, My only Son, Whom I love. I took His infinite worth and His majesty and His power, and I wrapped them in flesh and laid Him in a manger. Then I laid Him on the altar, and there I sacrificed Him—My Son—so that you could know the depths of My love for you. Oh, My child, did you know? The nails that pierced the hands of the Son, pierced the heart of the Father.

"O infinite God, the brightness of whose face is often shrouded from my mortal gaze, I thank Thee that Thou didst send Thy Son Jesus Christ to be a light in a dark world. O Christ, Though Light of Light, I thank Thee that in Thy most holy life Thou didst pierce the eternal

*mystery as with a great shaft of heavenly light, so that in seeing Thee
we see him whom no man hath seen at any time."*

—JOHN BAILLIE, *A Diary of Private Prayer*

AUGUST 22
Jesus,

Let my life be absorbed by Yours until Your life and my life
are one indissoluble whole. Let me be the vehicle for Your life in
my world.

*"On the first day of Pentecost He returned, not this time to be with
them externally—clothed with that sinless humanity that God had
prepared for Him, being conceived of the Holy Spirit in the womb of
Mary—but now to be in them, imparting to them His own divine
nature, clothing Himself with their humanity . . . He spoke with their
lips. He worked with their hands. This was the miracle of new birth,
and this remains the very heart of the gospel!"*

—MAJOR W. IAN THOMAS, *The Saving Life of Christ*

AUGUST 23
Jesus,

I am awed and forever grateful for the work You have done
for me. Now I hunger to know the fullness of the work You will
do in me.

*"His Life in me is creating desires that match God's will. 'It is God
who works in you to will . . . his good purpose' (Philippians 2:13).
He is expressing His desires through my desires so that when I ask
whatever I will, I am asking according to His will. He is causing my
will to come into alignment with His. To know God's will so that*

I will know how to pray with power, I must trust His Life operation in me."

—Jennifer Kennedy Dean, *Power Praying*

AUGUST 24
Child,

You were created for one purpose—to be the vessel into which I pour My life. Until you are a container for Me, you are not truly yourself. That sense of disconnectedness and alienation, the feeling that you are all alone and unable to fill the void in your center—that's your heart's cry. I have heard the cry of My people.

"When I am in him, I am in the Kingdom of God
And in the Fatherland of my Soul."

—Walter Rauschenbusch, from "The Little Gate to God"

AUGUST 25
Jesus,

Teach me to surrender to the power of Your life in me. Remind me that my efforts to help You only hinder You. Show me how to yield to Your work in me.

"The freer you are from exerting your own effort, the more quickly you will move toward your Lord.

"Why is this? Because there is a divine energy drawing you. When this divine energy is completely unhindered, He has complete liberty to draw you just as He pleases.

"Jesus Christ is the great magnet of your soul, but of your soul only. He will not draw the impurities and mixtures that are mingled with it. Any such impurities prevent His full power of attraction . . .

"Observe the ocean. The water in the ocean begins to evaporate. Then the vapor begins moving toward the sun. As the vapor leaves the earth, it is full of impurities; however, as it ascends, it becomes more refined and more purified.

"What did the vapor do? The vapor did nothing . . . The purifying took place as the vapor was drawn up into the heavens!"

—JEANNE GUYON, *Experiencing the Depths of Jesus Christ*

AUGUST 26
Father

Christ in me, shaping me in His image—my hope of glory! The only hope I have of fulfilling my destiny—to be the outshining of His brightness. Christ, my life.

"If you are to know the fullness of life in Christ, you are to appropriate the efficacy of what He is . . . Relate everything, moment by moment as it arises, to the adequacy of what He is in you, and assume that His adequacy will be operative . . . expose by faith every situation as it arises, to the all-sufficiency of the One who indwells you by His life. Can any situation possibly arise, in any circumstances, for which He is not adequate? Any pressure, promise, problem, responsibility or temptation for which the Lord Jesus Himself is not adequate? If He be truly God, there cannot be a single one!"

—MAJOR W. IAN THOMAS, *The Saving Life of Christ*

AUGUST 27
Jesus,

In You I find all that the Father offers. You are the storehouse of His riches. You are the coffer that holds His treasures. Everything He dispenses, He routes through You. All that belongs to the Father belongs to You. It is Yours to give. Apart from You, the riches of the Father cannot reach me. You are all I need. Having You, I have all.

"To pray is nothing more involved than to let Jesus into our needs. To pray is to give Jesus permission to employ His powers in the alleviation of our distress. To pray is to let Jesus glorify His name in the midst of our needs . . .

"To pray is nothing more involved than to open the door, giving Jesus access to our needs and permitting Him to exercise His own power in dealing with them."

—Ole Hallesby, *Prayer*

AUGUST 28
Spirit of the Living God,

You are the heat that fuses me into the body and makes me one with my brothers and sisters in Christ. As I yield to Your work, keeping in step with You, I find myself more and more living in peace with those around me.

"You were all called to travel on the same road and in the same direction, so stay together, both outwardly and inwardly. You have one Master, one faith, one baptism, one God and Father of all, who rules over all, works through all, and is present in all. Everything you are and think and do is permeated with Oneness" (Ephesians 4:4–6 The Message).

AUGUST 29
Father,

I release my whole personality and thought patterns and personality traits to Your Spirit in me. Reshape my desires and realign my inclinations and reform my will.

"The whole secret of prayer is found in these three words, 'In the Spirit.' It is the prayer that God the Holy Spirit inspires that God the Father answers . . . True prayer is prayer in the Spirit; that is, the prayer the Spirit inspires and directs . . . The Spirit knows the will of God. If I pray in the Spirit, and look to the Spirit to teach me God's will, He will lead me out in prayer along the line of that will, and give me faith that the prayer is to be answered."

—R. A. TORREY, *How to Pray*

AUGUST 30
Father,

I am Your temple. My purpose for being on the earth is to contain You. Until You fill me completely, I am not functioning at my capacity. Dwell in me richly.

"Remember again that the creature has no other end to his existence than to be a manifestor of the Creator—God in man, and God through man; and that therefore a human being is not true human until his is a temple of the Holy Spirit. Nothing can function except by the laws of its being; a car won't go unless its machinery words aright; and a man can never be a man unless he is a God-indwelt, God-controlled man, because men are not made to 'work' any other way."

—NORMAN P. GRUBB, *The Deep Things of God*

AUGUST 31
Father,

Because You have given me Your Spirit of prayer, before a desire has even become a conscious thought—before I have defined it and assigned words to it—You have prayed it through me. While it was no more than an inarticulate inner groaning, You expressed it to the Father. By the time I can speak it the answer is already prepared. Before I called, He heard and while I was yet speaking, He answered. "Before a word is on my tongue, you know it completely, O Lord" (Psalm 139:4).

"There come times when prayer pours forth in volumes and originality such as we cannot create. It rolls through us like a mighty tide. Our prayers are mingled with a vaster Word, a Word that at one time was made flesh. We pray, and yet it is not we who pray, but a Greater who prays in us . . . All we can say is, Prayer is taking place, and I am given to be in the orbit."

—Thomas R. Kelly, *A Testament of Devotion*

September

SEPTEMBER 1

Father,

By Your Holy Spirit, You make Jesus real in my present-tense experience. You speak things to my spiritual ears that my physical ears cannot hear. You take me into the deep things of God.

> *"I*
> *Seek in myself the things I hoped to say,*
> *But lo!, my wells are dry.*
> *Then, seeing me empty, you forsake*
> *The listener's role and through*
> *My dumb lips breathe and into utterance wake*
> *The thoughts I never knew."*
>
> —C. S. Lewis, *Letters to Malcolm*

SEPTEMBER 2

Father,

Fill me so completely with Your Spirit of Truth that no room is left for pretense. Stand guard over my heart—never let me hide behind religious words and rituals that mask a cold and empty center.

"The danger of religious formalities is that they may replace spiritual worship. This happened to the religious leaders of Jesus' day. They knew every detail of the ceremonial forms of worship, but when the intended object of their worship stood before them, they did not recognize Him. They had become so intent on the methods that they missed the truth . . . Outward forms of worship were intended to express true, inward worship. The danger is that they will disguise inward emptiness. The Holy Spirit is the guard against empty, surface religion."

> —Jennifer Kennedy Dean, *Heart's Cry*

SEPTEMBER 3

Holy Spirit,

Fire from heaven, consume me. Burn away the rubbish. Refine anything that survives the heat of your presence. Like the fire on the altar of sacrifice, never go out. Burn continually.

"On God's anvil. Perhaps you've been there. Melted down. Formless. Undone. . . . An instrument is useful only if it's in the right shape. A dull ax or bent screwdriver needs attention, and so do we. A good blacksmith keeps his tools in shape. So does God. Should God place you on his anvil, be thankful. It means he thinks you're still worth reshaping."

—Max Lucado, *On the Anvil*

SEPTEMBER 4

Spirit,

You are the promised power from on high. If you indwell me, then all the power of God indwells me. Teach me to get out of Your way, to stop hindering the flow of Your power. Draw my gaze away from my inability to focus on Your ability. You are able.

"I am a mighty power within you. The only time you are weak, My child, is when you choose to live in your own strength, not Mine. I give you the power to live in radiant intensity of joy and power and enthusiasm at the highest level of My Spirit's ability. From this moment on refer to weakness not as an enemy, for weakness open the way to My power."

—Marie Chapian, *His Thoughts Toward Me*

SEPTEMBER 5
Spirit,

Breath of God, my physical nature draws its life-sustaining resources from the earth. I breathe the earth's air. I eat the earth's food. I wear the earth's clothes. Earth is the proper environment for my physical nature. But my spiritual nature must draw its life-sustaining resources from heaven. I must breathe in Spirit; I must eat Spirit food; I must clothe myself in Christ. You are the point of contact between my spiritual nature housed on earth and my resources in heaven. You are my lifeline, my connection.

"Prayer is . . . the opening of a channel from your emptiness to God's fullness."

—E. STANLEY JONES, *Abundant Living*

SEPTEMBER 6
Spirit of God,

Show me the reality of the invisible world—the world of the Spirit. Open my eyes to the full spectrum of Your work in me, through me, and for me.

"Forbid, O Lord God, that my thoughts to-day should be wholly occupied with the world's passing show. Seeing that in Thy lovingkindness Thou hast given me the power to lift my mind to the contemplation of things unseen and eternal, forbid that I should remain content with the things of sense and time. Grant rather that each day may do something to strengthen my hold upon the unseen world, so to increase my sense of its reality, and so to attach my heart to its holy interests that, as the end of my earthly life draws

ever nearer, I may not grow to be a part of these fleeting earthly surroundings, but rather grow more and more conformed to the life of the world to come."

—JOHN BAILLIE, *A Diary of Private Prayer*

SEPTEMBER 7
My Child,

You are highly favored in heaven. You are privy to My secrets. I have decreed that you have the authority to access all of My riches. The forces of heaven are on alert, ready to spring into action at your call. I want to show you what belongs to you so that you will know what to ask for.

"We have not stopped praying for you. We continually ask God to fill you with the knowledge of his will through all the wisdom and understanding that the Spirit gives" (COLOSSIANS 1:9).

SEPTEMBER 8
Child,

I see your search. I know that you are conscientiously seeking My will. You want to live and pray with power. Relax. When you are resting in Me, My will finds you.

"Even the most ordinary idea, thought, or activity is often Him moving us to do His will. When we act on what seems to be a random choice, we often find ourselves right in the middle of 'the good works, which God prepared in advance for us to do' (Ephesians 2:10) . . . We walk continually in the flow of His will as He release His power from our spirit center into our personalities, intellects, will, emotions, and desires. He reproduces His will in us. We begin to understand faith

as rest, rather than faith as work. While our bodies are busy carrying out His will, our minds and emotions are resting in Him."

—Jennifer Kennedy Dean, *Riches Stored in Secret Places*

SEPTEMBER 9
Child,

You want Me to give you a detailed course of action. You think that if you could only know how and when, then you could have faith. But I will never do that because I am growing your capacity to trust Me. I am teaching you how to rely on your spiritual senses. I will show you the direction I am going, but not how I'll get there. Learn the adventure of watching My will unfold.

"Oh, the depth of the riches of the wisdom and knowledge of God! How unsearchable his judgments, and his paths beyond tracing out!" (Romans 11:33).

SEPTEMBER 10
Child,

I am clearly revealing My will to your spiritual senses. Learn to use them, and learn to trust them. They are in your spiritual genetic code; You inherited them from Me.

"When you were born into the physical world you were born with a set of physical senses. By means of these senses you interpret, under-stand, and interact with your physical world. . . . Faith is you God-given capacity to receive and act on spiritual knowledge. . . .You have learned that your physical senses are reliable. . . . When you were born into the kingdom of God, you were born with a set of spiritual senses. Your spiritual senses are the means by which you

know, understand, and respond to your spiritual world. . . . You
can be sure about the knowledge you receive by means of your
spiritual senses."

—Jennifer Kennedy Dean, *Live a Praying Life*

SEPTEMBER 11
Child,

I know that you feel insecure about your spiritual senses. I
know that to you they seem less real, less substantial, and less
reliable, than your physical senses. But that is only because you
have not practiced using them enough. I will only require of you
that which your spiritual senses are mature enough to perceive.
They will mature and sharpen with use.

"Faith will increase as your spiritual senses mature. When a baby
is born into the physical world, that baby has the sense of sight, but
cannot distinguish and identify shapes. The baby has the sense of
hearing, but cannot divide sounds into words and ascribe meaning to
them. The baby's senses have to mature over time and with practice.
It is the same with your spiritual senses. Knowing how to hear God
clearly and reliably is learned by the slow discipline of prayer and
obedience. God will guide you steadily and gently."

—Jennifer Kennedy Dean, *Live a Praying Life*

SEPTEMBER 12
Child,

My beloved, You choose how much of My will you really want
to know. You will know as much of My will as you are ready to
put into practice. You've already heard Me, but you've closed your
ears. When you act on what you know right now, I will take you
deeper. Today, when you hear My voice, do not harden your heart.

"And the longer and more beautiful the Lion sang, the harder Uncle Andrew tried to make himself believe that he could hear nothing but roaring. Now the trouble about trying to make yourself stupider than you really are is that you very often succeed. Uncle Andrew did. He soon did hear nothing but roaring in Aslan's song. Soon he couldn't have heard anything else even if he had wanted to."

—C. S. LEWIS, *The Magician's Nephew*

SEPTEMBER 13

Child,

If you want to hear Me, you have to trust My ability to speak to you.

"We find in [George Müeller's] journal frequent mention made of his spending two and three hours in prayer over the word for the feeding of his spiritual life. As the fruit of this, when he had need of strength and encouragement in prayer, the individual promises were not to him so many arguments from a book to be used with God, but living words which he had heard the Father's living voice speak to him, and which he could now bring to the Father in living faith."

—ANDREW MURRAY, *With Christ in the School of Prayer: Thoughts on Our Training for the Ministry of Intercession*

SEPTEMBER 14

Child,

You will find My will written in My Word, but only when the Living Word, My Son, is speaking it to you. Listen for My voice in My Word. Don't look for cut-and-dried, prepackaged formulas when I have fresh truth for you. Today, hear My voice.

"Prayer is an integral part of the cosmos. It is the spiritual 'token of exchange,' whereby the commodities of the unseen are brought into the possession of Man, who lives both in the unseen and the seen . . . The thought is tremendous. My friend, when you and I feel drawn to Prayer, it is God desirous of pouring forth His heart; the great depths of the thoughts of God—of His desires—seeking to find expression through such imperfect channels as you and me."

—G. Granger Fleming, *The Dynamic of All-Prayer*

SEPTEMBER 15
Child,

When you don't know My will, you do know My heart. You can be confident that My will in any situation is good, acceptable, and perfect. You do not have to be able to put My will into words in order to pray My will. My Son is teaching you the most powerful and effective prayer of all: "Let Your kingdom come; let Your will be done." You point to the need; I will apply My power.

"This power is so rich and so mobile that all we have to do when we pray is to point to the persons or things to which we desire to have this power applied, and He, the Lord of this power, will direct the necessary power to the desired place at once."

—Ole Hallesby, *Prayer*

SEPTEMBER 16
Child,

You can always know this about My will; it is My will to meet your needs and fulfill your desire. One way that I show you what I want to do is by allowing needs and desires into your life. By allowing them in, I am announcing to you My willingness—My eagerness—to apply My power in your life.

"What are the circumstances in your life that look overwhelming and impossible? Now place them against the backdrop of the amazing power and astonishing love of God. Do they look different now? Do you see them as they are? Every circumstance, every need, every desire is God's entry point into your life. Every difficulty is simply highlighting the exact place where God will apply His power. Every challenge or obstacle is God's opportunity to substantiate His promises. Problems are nothing more than labor pains as God brings about the birth of His vision."

—Jennifer Kennedy Dean, *Live a Praying Life in Adversity*

SEPTEMBER 17
My Children,

Though you may not feel it, you are all one. You cannot tear down another without diminishing yourself. When you build up another, you increase your own strength. Through you, My children born of My incorruptible seed and filled with My eternal life, I display My fullness.

"Encourage one another and build each other up" (1 Thessalonians 5:11).

SEPTEMBER 18
Little Flock,

Where among you is bitterness flourishing? Each of you, examine your own relationships within the body. As far as it is up to you, are you keeping peace? Are you protecting unity? Are your words promoting instruction? Or are they separating brothers? My purpose is to unite; Satan's purpose is to divide. Whose purpose are you establishing?

"God's desire is to provide safety, protection, and blessing in a company of believers. Satan's demons work overtime to provoke sins of slander, backbiting, gossip, hatred, and a host of other destructive attitudes and actions designed to destroy the body of Christ. As a result, God's people are isolated from each other and are left vulnerable to more insidious attacks by the enemy. And the enemy takes full advantage of these moments of discord in our relationships to generate resentments and bitterness that separate and destroy."

—RAY BEESON, *Create in Me a Clean Heart*

SEPTEMBER 19
Child,

My examining is making you uncomfortable. You want to justify yourself to Me—to tell Me how wronged you've been. Underlying all your sin crust is a core of fear that if you forgive your brother or sister completely, cancel out the debt owed, the wrong done to you may never be avenged and they will never be properly punished. You resent My mercy when it is directed toward someone who owes you an apology, and you are refusing to be the channel of My misdirected grace.

I do not hate You, God.
Please understand.
You are OK, A-One,
The Very Best,
second to none I know,
great and beyond
my criticism so
I say Amen
to You and all Your good
intentions—but
I might be right about
Your indiscretion in
forgiving folks

gladly and shamelessly
upon the least
evidence of regret.
I think
You carry love too far.

—Thomas John Carlisle, "Indiscretion," *You! Jonah!*

SEPTEMBER 20
Child,

Offspring of My Spirit, bitterness is not at home in you. I indwell you, and your life is not the natural environment for bitterness to root and grow. It is a weed, a fruit destroyer, an invader. It is sapping your joy and stunting your growth. Let Me have it, and I will uproot it. Unable to receive nourishment, it will wither and die. You will be free. Give Me your permission to begin the process.

"See to it that no one falls short of the grace of God and that no bitter root grows up to cause trouble and defile many" (Hebrews 12:15).

SEPTEMBER 21
Child,

My Well-watered Garden, I am beginning My uprooting project by digging underneath the root. Let Me show you what I found there. Give attention to Me while I shovel out the muck that nourished the root of bitterness. What made the offense offensive? What unhealed wound did it touch? What unsurrendered pride did it awaken? What insecurity did it unmask? What uncrucified flesh did it discover?

Sin
Crouching at my door
Deviously
Watching for the opportune moment
To pounce.
Sin
Probing for uncrucified life
Flesh with vital signs
To massage into viability
And master.
—JENNIFER KENNEDY DEAN

SEPTEMBER 22
Child,

Crucified One, now—deal the final death-blow to stubborn flesh that refuses to die. Don't hesitate because your emotions are not aligned with My purpose. Only I can change your heart, so don't try to do My job. Pray for the one who wronged you. Pray blessings and abundance for the one you are in the process of forgiving. Pour your anger and hurt out to Me, but pour My mercy out to your brother. I promise to give you opportunities to lift up and promote your offender. Do it, keep on doing it, and soon you will be as you should be—all glorious within.

Ensnared in our revenge
we die until
we claim the privilege
of sharing His
unerring mercy.
—THOMAS JOHN CARLISLE, "CAPTURED," *You! Jonah!*

SEPTEMBER 23
Child,

As a bridegroom rejoices over his bride, so I rejoice over you. A faithful wife—a wife of noble character—you are My treasure and the source of My joy. I will display you as My signet ring. Because of you, all will perceive and recognize My power and authority. You, bride, speak with wisdom; faithful instruction is on your tongue. Your words now are the overflow of your pure and poison-free heart.

"He is cheered and He beams with exceeding joy and takes pleasure in your presence. He has engraved a place for Himself in you and there He quietly rests in His love and affection for you. He cannot contain Himself at the thought of you and with the greatest of joy spins around wildly in anticipation over you, and has placed you above all other creations and in the highest place of His priorities. In fact, He shouts and sings in triumph, joyfully proclaiming the gladness of His heart in a song of rejoicing! All because of you!"
—DENNIS JERNIGAN, *Translation of Zephaniah 3:17*

SEPTEMBER 24
My Body,

When you see how ingeniously I have put you together, you will understand that the jealousy, turf guarding, and competition that define the world's interactions are a cell-destroying cancer when they invade My body. I have placed each of you into the body as a cell with a specific function that only you can fill. When you receive an instruction from the head, each of you responds to it according to your cell function. Your diverse reactions and differing responses are the coordinated action of the body at work.

"The final grounds of holy Fellowship are in God. Lives immersed and drowned in love, and know one another in Him, and know one another in love . . . Such lives have a common meeting-point; they

live in common joyous enslavement. They go back into a single Center where they are at home with Him and with one another. It is as if every soul had a final base, and that final base of every soul is one single Holy Ground, shared in by all . . . He is actively moving in all, co-ordinating those who are pliant to His will and suffusing them all with His glory and His joy."

—THOMAS R. KELLY, *A Testament of Devotion*

SEPTEMBER 25

Pass along the riches I invest in you. You are not to be reservoirs, but channels. I have placed the gifts of My Spirit among you. Gifts—not possessions. Things given are gifts; things hoarded are possessions. It is the act of giving away that transforms the thing.

"There are different kinds of gifts, but the same Spirit distributes them. There are different kinds of service, but the same Lord. There are different kinds of working, but in all of them and in everyone it is the same God at work. Now to each one the manifestation of the Spirit is given for the common good. . . . All these are the work of one and the same Spirit, and he distributes them to each one, just as he determines" (1 CORINTHIANS 12:4–11).

SEPTEMBER 26
Child,

I have given you the one essential element necessary for taking possession of all My promises: prayer. Prayer is the muscle structure that wields the weapons of your warfare and makes them operative. I have placed this secret weapon in your hands so that you can destroy the strongholds of the enemy and set captives free. The whole spiritual world is on notice. When you,

My church, announce with one voice My manifold wisdom, the spiritual realm must deploy accordingly.

"His intent was that now, through the church, the manifold wisdom of God should be made known to the rulers and authorities in the heavenly realms, according to his eternal purpose that he accomplished in Christ Jesus our Lord" (Ephesians 3:10–11).

SEPTEMBER 27
Citizen of My kingdom,

I have already transferred your citizenship from the world kingdom to My kingdom. The world kingdom is limited to the boundaries of time and space and senses: My kingdom has no limits—not boundaries imposed by geography, no restraints dictated by time, no finite apprehension of truth narrowly defined by sense knowledge. You are now a citizen and inhabitant of the kingdom of power and eternity. The riches of My kingdom are at your disposal. Seek the kingdom—study the landscape, learn the governing principles, become acquainted with the natural resources—so that you can make full use of your citizenship.

"But seek first his kingdom and his righteousness, and all these things will be given to you as well" (Matthew 6:33).

SEPTEMBER 28
Child,

Heir to My Riches, understand this kingdom principle: because you are fully instated as a citizen of My kingdom, you never have to worry about anything. All the energy that citizens of the world kingdom expend scurrying after earthly supplies, you will put to eternal use. Everything you need to operate in the earthly environment, I have already set aside and earmarked for you. It is yours. Turn your energy and your passion to seeking and possessing the kingdom riches.

"A settled peace . . . is the most frequent experience of those who have trod the path of relinquishment . . . Frequently we hold on so tightly to the good that we do know that we cannot receive the greater good that we do not know. God has to help us let go of our tiny vision in order to release the greater good his has in store for us."

—Richard J. Foster, *Prayer*

SEPTEMBER 29
Child,

You are a Joint heir with My Son; I have given you the legal designation of joint heir with Jesus. Do you know what that entails? It means that you and Jesus are copossessors of My kingdom. Joint heirs do not split the inheritance between them; they jointly own everything. Whatever I have given to Jesus belongs to you! Think about it—I loved you so much that I did not withhold My only and deeply beloved Son. I have given you the very core of My heart—the One most precious to Me and most valued by Me. Would I, then, withhold anything from you? Have no anxiety about anything.

"I meet today, today. I do not telescope all next week into today. I clip off all my engagements one by one as a person clips off coupons . . . I do not take any worries to bed with me. Bishop Quayle tells of lying awake, trying to hold the world together by his worrying, when God said, 'Now, William, you go to sleep and I'll sit up.'"

—E. Stanley Jones, *Abundant Living*

SEPTEMBER 30
Child,

I know all about the situation that is worrying you right now. I knew about it before you did. Believe Me, when I tell you it is finished. You prayers are bringing the finished work out of the spiritual realm to establish it in the material realm. You do not see the finished work in the earth's environment yet, but earth is not your home. Do you know why you are having difficulty believing right now? Because you have only looked at the situation in the artificial light of the earth kingdom. Earth kingdom's light only shows up the need. Bring it to Me. Spend time with Me in your true kingdom. Look at it in the Eternal Light. I will blot out the need and illumine the only supply. Come!

"The real difficulty is . . . to adapt one's steady beliefs about tribulation to this particular tribulation: for the particular, when it arrives, always seems so peculiarly intolerable."

—C. S. Lewis, *Letters of C. S. Lewis*

October

OCTOBER 1
Child,

Beloved, I am watching over you continually. My eye never wanders. I never fall asleep. You are *always* in My care. You do not have to perform rituals that will attract My attention. You have My full attention every minute of every day. You cannot ask more of Me than I am longing to give. Ask! Ask! And keep on asking!

"When I was too busy with my petty concerns to remember Thee, Thou with a universe to govern wert not too busy to remember me."
—JOHN BAILLIE, *A Diary of Private Prayer*

OCTOBER 2
Child,

I'm here. I'm ready. Just turn to Me. Everything is ready and waiting. Seeking Me is never in vain. If I am drawing you to Me in the midst of your longing, it is because I have what you need. Everything you need is right here in My hand, and My hand is held out to you. I long to give. I long to bless. I delight in lavishing you with My love, entering right into your messy circumstances, wading into your deep waters. My hands are full of heaven's riches.

"I publicly proclaim bold promises. I do not whisper obscurities in some dark corner. I would not have told the people of Israel to seek me if I could not be found. I, the LORD, speak only what is true and declare only what is right" (ISAIAH 45:19 NLT).

OCTOBER 3
Child,

You must remember that what takes you by surprise does not take Me by surprise. Anything that touches you has been scrutinized and carefully evaluated by Me. You are one of My honored and cherished kingdom dwellers. You are under My protection. It only reaches you if I have determined that the pain it causes will be outweighed by the glory it brings. I have not let it touch you until I have prepared you, prepared every circumstance, put every piece in place. The situation that is causing you pain and anxiety right now is not a punishment; it is not because you have not found the correct prayer method. Cooperate with Me, and you will find the eternal weight of glory secreted away in your situation.

"That is the secret! You co-operate with the immediate inevitable because you know that in and through things God's will is being worked out, and that Will wills your good."

—E. STANLEY JONES, *Abundant Living*

OCTOBER 4
Child,

As you learn more how to live in My kingdom while existing on the earth, you are noticing changes—some so subtle that they've been in place for some time before you recognize them. Do you know why? It's because your earthbound will, the will that your flesh birthed, cannot thrive in the environment of My kingdom. My kingdom is not its natural habitat. As the natural course of things, your little will is dying and being replaced by My perfect will.

"Little by little we are changed by this daily crucifixion of the will. Changed, not like a tornado changes things, but like a grain of sand in an oyster changes things . . . Please remember, we are dealing with the crucifixion of the will, not the obliteration of the will. Crucifixion always has resurrection tied to it. God is not destroying the will but transforming it so that over a process of time and experience we can freely will what God wills."

—RICHARD J. FOSTER, *Prayer*

OCTOBER 5
My Child,

The defining attribute of My kingdom is joy. This is not a solemn place. Here, in My house, is a banquet, a forever celebration—dancing and singing and laughter. As you are making the transition from one kingdom to the other, as your eyes are adjusting to a new light, you may not have realized the joy yet. But come on! Just ahead of you, just a few more steps, you are almost to the banquet hall.

Leaving old
Embracing New
Escaping boundaries
Embracing Infinity
Fleeing darkness
Embracing Light
Forsaking emptiness
Embracing Joy
—JENNIFER KENNEDY DEAN

OCTOBER 6
Child,

When you were born into My kingdom, My kingdom was born into you. My kingdom is flowing out of you onto the earth. Little you—you are the leaven that will leaven the whole loaf; you are the mustard seed that will grow to a tree-sized plant. Don't look at your littleness, look at My greatness. Every act of faith and obedience puts My kingdom into the earth environment. Every time you speak My name, every time you act My love, every time you tell My truth—kingdom light overcomes earth darkness. In that place at that time, My kingdom comes.

"The true prophetic message always calls us to a spiritual defiance of the world as it is now. Our prayer, to the extent that it is fully authentic, undermines the status quo. It is a spiritual underground resistance movement."

—RICHARD J. FOSTER, *Prayer*

OCTOBER 7
Child,

Before you were born into My kingdom, while I was waiting for your arrival, I prepared for you. I laid the table and prepared the fatted calf. I made you a robe and fitted a ring for your finger. I anticipated your entrance with such joy. I could hardly wait until you got here. I kept whispering to you—telling you what I had prepared for you. When I saw you coming, I was so excited that I ran to meet you and led you home. It gives Me deep pleasure to see you use and enjoy your inheritance.

"Try and see a Mother preparing birthday or Christmas delights for her child—the while her Mother-heart sings: 'Will she not love that? How she will love this!' and anticipates the rapture of her child, her own heart full of the tenderest joy. Where did the Mother learn all this preparation—joy? From Me—a faint echo this of My preparation— joy. Try to see this as plans unfold of My preparing."

—TWO LISTENERS, *God Calling*

OCTOBER 8
Father,

I embrace my destiny—to become the Son's reflection, just as the Son is the Father's reflection. I say yes to the transforming power of His life in me. I yield to His work as He moves me from one degree of glory to the next. What higher ambition could I have? Why would I serve any other ambition with more passion than I pursue this high call?

"We all, who with unveiled faces reflect the Lord's glory, are being transformed into his likeness with ever-increasing glory, which comes from the Lord, who is the Spirit" (2 CORINTHIANS 3:18).

OCTOBER 9
Child,

I am sculpting you into a perfect expression of Myself in the world. You are My work of art. I take such time and care with you—chiseling, sanding, shaping. When you are finished, you will be a masterpiece, worthy of bearing My name. When you resist My work, you distort My expression.

"Every sin is the distortion of an energy breathed into us . . . We poison the wine as He decants it into us; murder a melody he would play with us as the instrument. We caricature the self-portrait He would paint. Hence all sin, whatever else it is, is sacrilege."
—C. S. LEWIS, *Letters to Malcolm: Chiefly on Prayer*

OCTOBER 10
Child,

You are My self-portrait, your inner life is the canvas on which I am painting. I am painting you against the background of eternity. It brings out your best features. Day by day, brush stroke by brush stroke, I am perfecting My work. When I am finished, it will be like looking in a mirror.

"What is the process by which we come to reflect Him? 'And we who with unveiled faces all reflect the Lord's glory, are being changed into his likeness with ever-increasing glory, which comes from the Lord, who is the Spirit' (2 Corinthians 3:18). . . . Paul is telling us that because we are in the Lord's presence, we [like Moses] reflect His glory as a mirror reflects an image . . . How does a mirror reflect? It absorbs light bouncing off an object and projects it back in exactly the same configuration. It absorbs and reflects. As we absorb Him . . . we are being changed into an exact reflection of Him. We are being transformed—changed from the inside out; structurally changed. . . . How is this changing being accomplished? 'Which comes from the Lord, who is the Spirit.' The Spirit is doing the changing as we continue in His presence."

—Jennifer Kennedy Dean, *Live a Praying Life*

OCTOBER 11

Child,

My Image, it is My job to transform you; it is your job to be accessible. At first, you will need to discipline yourself and consciously remember to keep your life open to Me. Later, with practice, it will become your holy habit. It will not always be work—soon it will be rest. Put in the continual will-surrendering work so that you can make it to the more mature level rest. Make every effort to enter My rest (Hebrews 4:11).

"But longer discipline in this inward prayer will establish more enduring upreachings of praise and submission and relaxed listening in the depths, unworded but habitual orientation of all one's self about Him who is the Focus. The process is much simpler now. Little glances, quiet breathings of submission and invitation suffice. Behind the foreground of the words continuous background of heavenly orientation, as all the currents of our being set toward Him. Through the shimmering light of Divine Presence we look out upon the world, and in its turmoil and fitfulness, we may be given to respond in some

increased measure, in ways dimly suggestive of the Son of Man."

—Thomas R. Kelly, A Testament of Devotion

OCTOBER 12
Child,

Clay in My Hands, I need soft clay. Each act of disobedience hardens your heart toward Me. Sin by sin, if unconfessed, you grow more brittle and less moldable. Each time your refuse My voice, My voice becomes harder for you to hear. But each act of obedience softens you. Obedience by obedience, you become softer in My hands, easier to mold. I can make you into something altogether new.

"There is such a thing as coming into such sweet relation to the will of God that we are fused into oneness with it. His will becomes ours, and He gladly sets us free to carry out our own wishes—they really being His first and then ours."

—G. Granger Fleming, The Dynamic of All-Prayer

OCTOBER 13
Child,

You are My Heart Reflection. Don't feel discouraged because you seem to be meeting the same sin pattern in yourself over and over again. You think I must be becoming impatient—that I must be disappointed in you because you have to confess the same sin over and over again. I don't grow weary. I'm not disappointed. You see, I knew all along it was there. I want you to recognize its hold and long for freedom from it. I won't let you bury it or disguise it anymore. This experience is a cleansing process. Part of My cleansing process is a desert walk: you have to be convinced of your own inability. The second part is living in the Promised

Land: you finally turn away from your own efforts and look to My power. I am able to perfect what concerns you.

A heart like Yours, my one desire.
Do Your work, Refiner's Fire.
—Jennifer Kennedy Dean

OCTOBER 14
Child,

My tabernacle, as you yield to Me, I am refocusing your passions and refining your vision. You look more like Me every day.

"Just as the moon cannot be reflected well on a restless sea, so God cannot get to an unquiet mind. 'Be still, and know'; be unstill and you do not know—God cannot get to you. In the stillness the prayer itself may be corrected. For God does not only answer prayer; He also corrects prayer and makes it more answerable. One night I bowed my head in silent prayer before a sermon and whispered to God, 'O God, help me.' Very quickly came back the reply: 'I will do something better; I will use you.' That amendment was decidedly better. I was asking God to help me—I was the center; I was calling to God for my own purposes. But 'I will use you' meant I was not the center; something beyond me was the center and I was only the instrument of that purpose beyond myself. God's answer shifted the whole center of gravity of the prayer."

—E. Stanley Jones, Abundant Living

OCTOBER 15
Child,

Work of My Hands, I know that sometimes My sculpting hurts. Sometimes you feel as though you are looking less like

Me rather than more like Me. Don't worry. It's just a stage in the sculpting process. There are intervals in the work of precisely shaping you during which you look like a shapeless, formless lump of clay. Your old shape has been destroyed, but your new shape has not yet emerged. Don't give up. I am the Master Artist. Those are My hands you feel squeezing you and pushing you. I know exactly what I'm doing.

Infinite Patience
Meticulous attention to detail
Consuming focus
Perfectionist
Master Potter
Lovingly shaping
Vessels of His Mercy
—JENNIFER KENNEDY DEAN

OCTOBER 16
Child,

Vessel of My Life, don't be discouraged because it seems I am not answering your prayers. You are allowing your disappointment to give you a spiritual inferiority complex. You are beginning to doubt that I care at all. "Maybe they're right after all," you say. "Maybe God is too big to get involved in my little affairs. Maybe He is too busy for me." No child, every step you take and every thought you think are infinitely precious to Me. Right now is a season for learning to move deeper into the kingdom. I am teaching you the difference between the desires of the moment and the desires of your heart.

"Rows of beautiful trees were laid low in a storm. Reason? The water was too near the surface; so the trees did not have to put their roots deep down to find water; hence the tragedy. God may deny us a

surface answer in order to get us to put our roots deeper into eternal reality, so that tin some future storm we shall be unmoved."

—E. STANLEY JONES, *Abundant Living*

OCTOBER 17
Child,

Blessed One, part of the shaping is done by fire. But it is not a destroying fire; it is a cleansing fire. When you walk through it, it will not burn you. It will refine you. I am in the fire. It is going to burn away the earth stuff still clinging to you. It is going to set the work I have finished so that the shape is stable. Once you've walked through the fire and have seen for yourself that you are invulnerable to any power except Mine, you will be My fearless warrior.

"'Hero!' Mercie called . . . 'You are wondering what is wrong with Amanda. She is trying to bear her own guilt; that is a burden too heavy for anyone to carry." . . .

"'What will help her? Will she ever be herself?' [Hero asked.]

"[Mercie answered,] 'The King can help her. When we walk through the Sacred Flames, we always become what we really are. Amanda needs to go back to the Great Celebration. The cure for disobedience is to obey again.'

"Hero thought about his own unfulfilled vow. 'Is she afraid of the Sacred Flames?' he asked.

"The old woman looked at him . . . 'You are afraid of the Sacred Flames. Amanda is afraid of the King. She is afraid he will banish her, because she has been faithless.'

"Mercie looked far away, as though she was seeing something far off. 'We all have to walk through what we fear most in order to gain the thing we want most. What do you want most, Hero?'"

—DAVID AND KAREN MAINS, *Tales of the Kingdom*

OCTOBER 18,

You are My Holy of Holies. Don't be shocked that I would call you My holy of holies. That's exactly what you are. You are the place of My presence. My law and My power are in you. You have been cleansed by the blood sprinkling. My *Shekinah* glory burns in you. You are My most holy place. All My shaping and molding is for one purpose: to display My splendor through you, to make you holy on the outside so that the inner chamber of My presence will be seen.

"When in the presence of God lowliness of heart has become, not a posture we assume for a time, when we think of Him, or pray to Him, but the very spirit of our life, it will manifest itself in all our bearings towards our brethren . . . the insignificances of daily life are the importances and tests of eternity, because they prove what really is the spirit that possesses us."

—Andrew Murray, *Humility: The Beauty of Holiness*

OCTOBER 19
Father,

Put Your world on my heart. Cause me to love with Your self-giving passion. Let me see through Your eyes. Teach me how to recognize the pain hidden by pretense, the sorrow disguised by swagger. Move me with the plight of a decaying world—a world for whom You gave all.

"For God so loved the world that he gave his one and only Son, that whoever believes in him shall not perish but have eternal life" (John 3:16).

OCTOBER 20
Savior,

I know that I cannot invite You into my life and leave a dying world out. It is through me that You want to reach out, beseech the lost, love the hurting, supply the needy. Until Your agenda is mine, I am not unreservedly surrendered. Make me Yours.

"And he has committed to us the message of reconciliation. We are therefore Christ's ambassadors, as though God were making his appeal through us. We implore you on Christ's behalf: Be reconciled to God. God made him who had no sin to be sin for us, so that in him we might become the righteousness of God" (2 CORINTHIANS 5:19–21).

OCTOBER 21
Father,

You are everywhere I look. You have transformed my seeing. I am dying to my littleness so that I can live in Your greatness. Now You look out from my eyes and see my world. You look with tenderness and patience and unfathomable love. Little by little, I'm seeing as You see.

"There stands the world of struggling, sinful, earth-blinded men and nations . . . all lapped in the tender, persuading Love at the Center . . . Marks of glory are upon all things, and the marks are cruciform and blood-stained."
—THOMAS R. KELLY, *A Testament of Devotion*

OCTOBER 22
Father,

As You hold me close to Your heart, our hearts are becoming one. In Your presence, my sin-altered priorities are being restored to their eternal position.

"Guidance of life by the Light within . . . begins first of all in a mass revision of our total reaction to the world. Worshipping in the light we become new creatures, making wholly new and astonishing responses to the entire outer setting of life . . . The dynamic illumination from the deeper level is shed upon the judgments of the surface level, and lo, the 'former things are passed away, behold, they are become new.' Paradoxically, this total instruction proceeds in two opposing directions at once. We are torn loose from the earthly attachments and ambitions . . . And we are quickened to a divine but painful concern for the world . . . He plucks the world out of our hearts, loosening the chains of attachment. And He hurls the world into our heart, where we and He together carry it in infinitely tender love."

—THOMAS R. KELLY, *A Testament of Devotion*

OCTOBER 23
Father,

Loving Lord, let me be the censer that spreads the aroma of the knowledge of You everywhere. As if I were an alabaster jar filled with priceless perfume, break me. Empty me out at Your feet. Let the fragrance of You fill the world around me.

"The true prophetic message always calls us to stretch our arms out wide and embrace the whole world. In a holy boldness we cover the earth with the grace and mercy of God."

—RICHARD J. FOSTER, *Prayer*

OCTOBER 24
Father,

Creator, I give myself unreservedly to You. My life is on Your altar, waiting to be consumed by the fire from heaven. I do not belong to myself; I belong to You. Count me among Your treasured possessions. Do through me what You will, when You will, how You will.

"Take your everyday, ordinary life—your sleeping, eating, going-to-work, and walking-around life—and place it before God as an offering" (ROMANS 12:1–2 THE MESSAGE).

OCTOBER 25
Father,

World Lover, You have my permission to love Your world through me anytime You want.

If I open my heart to You
Then I have opened my heart to the world.
Disturbing thought.
The world may not be respectful
Of my schedule
Or the demands on my
Energy.
The world may clamor for my attention
At inconvenient times.
Are there ever intervals
When the world
Is not on Your heart?
Perhaps we could arrange to meet

Then—
Just the two of us.
—Jennifer Kennedy Dean, "The Inconveniences of Love"

OCTOBER 26

Father,

God of All Comfort, Your perfectly restored, resurrection body retained its wounds. The hand You stretch out to the world is a wounded hand. Give me the courage to heal out of my own woundedness. Let me pass along the miraculous balm that took the pain out of my injuries.

Keep open
to pain
his hers theirs
as well as yours
Threshold
deep wide
for untranquilized
empathizers
Agony
can create capacity
to respond
in kind
Acute heartbreak
walks back
to gather pieces
bandage wounds
Sensitive
to all living
all suffering
let mercy thrive

—Thomas John Carlisle, "Passion for Compassion," *You! Jonah!*

OCTOBER 27
Father,

All-seeing One, give me x-ray eyes to see through the walls in the lives of my neighbors, my family members, and the strangers on my way. Give me grace to envision Your finished work even in its beginning stages.

"[Jesus] stubbornly rejected their surface appearances. He ignored the nicely calculated probabilities of society's judgment of what one might expect of them. He penetrated even the heavy wrappings of what they had themselves settled for in their lives and pierced through to what in their deepest yearnings they still longed to become. He drew this out, confirmed it, [they] acknowledged it and accepted it. He answered expectantly to that of God in each of them and they felt and responded to the quickening."

—Douglas V. Steere, *On Listening to Another*

OCTOBER 28
Jesus,

The only remedy for my tendency to fall again into sinful behaviors and habits is the all-surpassing beauty of You. Teach me to maximize my pleasure in You. To find my deepest joy in Your presence. As my heart habituates to the beautiful reality of the spiritual realm, and of Your nearness, the appeal of my sins loses its hold. I find myself not sinning in ways I used to, not because of my tremendous willpower, but because sin is losing its luster. What can compare to You?

"A being terrified with fears of wrath and seeing the dismal consequences of sin has in itself no tendency to wean the heart from sin:

for true weanedness from sin doesn't consist in being afraid of the mischief that will follow from sin, but in hating sin itself, and doesn't arise from a sight of the dreadful consequences of sin, but from a sight of the odiousness of sin in its own nature. . . . For a man to meet with many worldly losses and disappointments has in itself no tendency to true weanedness from the world, because true weanedness from the world doesn't consist in being beat off from the world by the affliction of it, but a being drawn off by the sight of something better"
—JONATHAN EDWARDS, *Religious Affections*

OCTOBER 29

Jesus,

I hear You telling me to be continually filled to capacity with Your Spirit instead of being drunk on wine. Like overindulgence in wine removes a person's boundaries and takes over the personality, turning them into someone else—You seem to be saying that I should be that fully given over to Your Spirit. When Your Spirit fills every inch of me, I become another version of myself. Bold, fearless, audacious—under Your Spirit's guidance. Under the influence of wine, foolishness is exhibited, but under the influence of Your Spirit, wisdom is the watchword. I can live in a power not my own. I can exhibit You without restraint. Fill me now and always.

"Be very careful, then, how you live—not as unwise but as wise, making the most of every opportunity, because the days are evil. Therefore do not be foolish, but understand what the Lord's will is. Do not get drunk on wine, which leads to debauchery. Instead, be filled with the Spirit, speaking to one another with psalms, hymns, and songs from the Spirit. Sing and make music from your heart to the Lord, always giving thanks to God the Father for everything, in the name of our Lord Jesus Christ" (EPHESIANS 5:15–20).

OCTOBER 30

Child,

Being filled with My Spirit is not an experience, but a relationship. Everything I have called you to is about the living, indwelling Jesus. He is the Author and Finisher, the Beginning and the End, He is the Life. My Spirit is the delivery system for His life. Receive all of Jesus into the nooks and crannies of your being through My Spirit. Let Him flow into the dry places, into the wounded spots, into the junk rooms and storage closets. Give Him full access.

"O Holy Spirit, descend plentifully into my heart. Enlighten the dark corners of this neglected dwelling and scatter there Thy cheerful beams."

—Augustine

OCTOBER 31

Child,

To be filled with My Spirit is to be filled not only in every part of your life, but also in every *moment* of your life. As you walk out your life minute by minute, a step at a time, you are flooded with My Spirit. He is delivering the present Jesus into every juncture of your experiences. Whether you turn right or left, there He is. Nothing is too insignificant to count on His powerful, filling presence—little decisions or big, passing encounters or significant interactions. My Spirit is equally present and powerful in any circumstance that finds you.

"To the individual believer . . . indwelt by the Holy Spirit . . . there is granted the direct impression of the Spirit of God on the spirit of man, imparting the knowledge of his will in matters of the smallest and greatest importance. This has to be sought and waited for."

—G. Campbell Morgan

November

NOVEMBER 1
Child,

I am not satisfied to possess *some* of you, or *a portion* of you, or even *most of* you. I have so much to give that it requires *all* of you to hold it.

"Amplius—broader, fuller, wider. That is God's perpetual word to us in relation to filling of the Holy Spirit. We can never have enough to satisfy His yearning desire. When we have apprehended most, there are always unexplored oceans and continents beyond."
—F. B. Meyer, *Through Fire and Flood*

NOVEMBER 2
Child,

I have never held anything back from you. The instant you received Me into your life, you got all of Me. Everything it would take to secure your salvation, I gave freely. Everything it takes to work that salvation out in your experience, I give freely. I long for you to be as fully committed to Me as I am to you. Let your heart soak for a while in the magnitude of My love for you. Nothing held back, all in.

"Jesus held nothing back in securing your salvation, and holds nothing back in expressing His life in you. He could have lived for all eternity without once experiencing death's direct hit. He could have kept His distance and avoided taking all our pain and death into Himself. He loves you with reckless abandon."
—Jennifer Kennedy Dean, *Altar'd*

NOVEMBER 3
Child,

Let Me prepare your heart to receive the seed of My word. I want My word to put down roots in you and grow lush, healthy fruit. I have to prepare the ground. I have to plow up those areas that are fallow. I have to stir things up to move the rocky topsoil and get to the rich and fertile ground. Don't panic. The upending, the turning things inside out—it's Me. I don't plow ground I don't intend to plant. A harvest is headed your way. Surrender to the work I'm doing.

"When a farmer plows for planting, does he plow continually? Does he keep on breaking up and working the soil? When he has leveled the surface, does he not sow caraway and scatter cumin? Does he not plant wheat in its place, barley in its plot, and spelt in its field?" (ISAIAH 28:24–25).

NOVEMBER 4
Child,

The pain you're feeling right now won't last. I have transformed all pain to have a redemptive outcome. It is doing a beneficial work. I'm holding you and healing you. You are not in this alone. Look at the Cross. This is what I have done: I have turned all endings into beginnings.

"Do you see that the crucifixion that God is bringing into your life has a purpose? He is emptying you of flesh in order to fill you with Himself. He is cleansing you of sin in order to make room for His glory. He is in the process of giving you a steadfast, undivided heart to replace your old, unsteady, unreliable heart. The process has some pain inherent in it, but when you recognize that the pain is a means to an end, it takes on a new meaning for you."

—JENNIFER KENNEDY DEAN, *Altar'd*

NOVEMBER 5
Child,

I am gentle and tender in My dealings with you and with those you love. I'm so careful over you that My word paints a picture: I wouldn't break a bruised reed, or snuff out a smoldering wick. The most fragile are safe with Me: a bruised reed—still standing on the outside, but deeply wounded on the inside, deep injury, like the injury to the body's internal organs, bleeding and dying, but nothing of that death showing on the outside. It would just take the smallest gust of wind—maybe the stirring of the air as a person walked by unheeding—and the reed would break. And so I strike a defender's pose. I place Myself between that fragile one and any small disturbance that would break it. Any force arrayed against it will find it has a fierce and unassailable Defender. A smoldering wick? What do I do to keep a smoldering wick from going out? Once a bright flame, now barely discernible, I cup My palms around it. That flickering, smoldering wick is surrounded and hidden in the palms of My hands.

"A bruised reed he will not break, and a smoldering wick he will not snuff out" (ISAIAH 42:3).

NOVEMBER 6
Father,

Your grand eternal plan is staggering. What You have done to set it in motion and to secure its outcome is astounding. But to think that Your way of carrying that plan forward is by using such frail and faulty ones as me—that is beyond belief. We're Your plan A, and there is no plan B. Your plan depends on me being exactly where I am, in the middle of the lives You've connected to mine. Use everything about me, Father. I'm Yours.

"And seeing that it is Thy gracious will to make use even of such weak human instruments in the fulfilment of Thy mighty purpose for the world, let my life to-day be the channel through which some little portion of Thy divine love and pity may reach the lives that are nearest to my own."

—JOHN BAILLIE, *A Diary of Private Prayer*

NOVEMBER 7
Child,

Every blessing I have bestowed on you—physical, material, financial, spiritual—has but one purpose. It is to be used to bless others. Lose your life for My sake, and you will have found it. You aren't meant to store up and when you do, everything I have given you wears out and wears you out. It loses its flavor. Like the manna I provided in the wilderness, when you try to stockpile My blessings, they get moldy and useless. When you live generously, you live joyfully.

"Then Moses said to them, 'No one is to keep any of it until morning.' However, some of them paid no attention to Moses; they kept part of it until morning, but it was full of maggots and began to smell" (EXODUS 16:19–20).

NOVEMBER 8
Father,

How quick I am to see the failings of others, and slow to recognize my own. How easily I defend and explain away my own wrongs, but hold others to a higher standard. How easily

I can become consumed with my own struggles and ignore those of others. How effortlessly I fall into self-pity and soon find myself the center of my universe with no thought for anyone else. My supposed calamity grows in my imagination until it blocks the light and hides any other thought. Save Me, Father, from the great burden of self-focused living.

"Therefore if you have any encouragement from being united with Christ, if any comfort from his love, if any common sharing in the Spirit, if any tenderness and compassion, then make my joy complete by being like-minded, having the same love, being one in spirit and of one mind. Do nothing out of selfish ambition or vain conceit. Rather, in humility value others above yourselves, not looking to your own interests but each of you to the interests of the others. In your relationships with one another, have the same mindset as Christ Jesus" (PHILIPPIANS 2:1–5).

NOVEMBER 9
Father,

You know what lies ahead. You are working in my life today, and arranging situations and circumstances that will make sense in the future. When I see then what You see now, I will know that You are never wasting time or experience. You are efficiently working in my life for the highest good and best outcome. You are not dragging things out. You are timing things strategically. I take hold of these truths and carry them with me as I walk into what comes next.

"All the days ordained for me were written in your book before one of them came to be" (PSALM 139:16).

NOVEMBER 10
Child,

Don't lean on your own understanding. I don't mean that I don't want you to understand. I very much want you to understand. I have created you with an intellect and a brain that can understand. But don't lean on your own understanding. Don't go by the best you can figure out. Let My Spirit impart understanding and park it in your brain. I can make a direct deposit from My mind into yours, but only if you are willing to lay aside the way you think and reason to receive the way I think and reason.

"For the LORD gives wisdom; from his mouth come knowledge and understanding. . . . Then you will understand what is right and just and fair—every good path. For wisdom will enter your heart, and knowledge will be pleasant to your soul. Discretion will protect you, and understanding will guard you" (PROVERBS 2:6, 9–11).

NOVEMBER 11
Child,

Providing for you is not a stretch for Me. I know that it looks bleak because you look around you and you see nothing to give you hope. That's when you just believe Me. If you could take some comfort because you could see some possibilities, then you would be putting faith in what you can see. There is nothing supernatural about that. I want you to use this situation to learn at a deeper level what you have learned before—faith is being sure of what you do not see (Hebrews 11:1). I'm speaking faith into you. Just listen. Faith comes by hearing My word, so let Me speak truth to you (Romans 10:17). Before you grow in faith, faith will grow in you. How do you see Me right now? Hand wringing? Pacing the floor? Struggling to figure it out? Or can you see that I'm at rest. Join Me in My rest.

"In peace I will lie down and sleep, for you alone, LORD, make me dwell in safety" (PSALM 4:8).

NOVEMBER 12
Father,

Your Word is a rich treasure trove that is never fully mined. Every day You show me something in Your Word that thrills my heart and awakens new faith. It energizes me anew. I know that Your Word is more than words on pages penned in years gone by. It speaks loud and clear to me in the middle of my every day walking-around life. Your Spirit brings to mind words I've known for a long time, and suddenly they are new and amazing because Your Spirit has breathed life into them. It is one of the most authentic proofs to me that You are powerful and present. The way Your Word speaks and speaks and then speaks again.

"I rejoice in your promise like one who finds great spoil" (PSALM 119:162).

NOVEMBER 13
Child,

Today, express your worship in your body's posture. Position your body differently. Kneel, or bow, or lay prostrate on the ground. Let the eyes of your heart see My presence. Use the visual brain I have designed—let it see the realities I have carefully described in My Word. See Me, high and lifted up. Use music. Music opens the floodgates of worship and brings your emotions to the surface. Worship Me with your whole heart and soul. You don't have to be careful about appearing silly. No one else is watching. It's just us.

The whole earth is filled with awe at your wonders; where morning dawns, where evening fades, you call forth songs of joy" (Psalm 65:8).

NOVEMBER 14

Child,

Today, offer Me everything about you, deliberately, thoughtfully, intentionally. Let My Spirit guide your thoughts. Start at your head, then your eyes, mouth, ears, and so on. Stop at each place My Spirit pinpoints. Lay each thing He prompts you about on My altar. Listen to how He guides you.

"The goal is not simply the imitation of Christ, but the manifestation of Christ. The purpose of Christ in us is Christ through us. This involves obedience and surrender."

—Jennifer Kennedy Dean, *Altar'd*

NOVEMBER 15

Child,

Live bowed before Me. The times of worship feed the life of worship. You can't always be in a bodily posture of worship. You can't always be singing praises aloud. But you can always be worshipping. The truest expression of worship is your obedience to My every whisper. Every time you obey, it delights Me. I see you trusting Me and putting confidence in My voice. I know you will live more and more in the fullness I have for you. I love your obedience.

"You are my portion, Lord; I have promised to obey your words. I have sought your face with all my heart; be gracious to me according to your promise. I have considered my ways and have turned my steps

to your statutes. I will hasten and not delay to obey your commands"
(PSALM 119:57–60).

NOVEMBER 16
Child,

Don't say cutting, unkind words. Don't say them *to* anyone, and don't say them *about* anyone. Did you assume that harsh words spoken didn't count if the person about whom you spoke them didn't experience them? You experienced them, and the anger and pettiness that formed that opinion settled deeper within you. The person to whom you spoke them experienced them, and now that person picked up your bitterness and has to carry it around as a burden. When you find yourself in a situation, and you feel free to speak critically about someone else, regroup. In your mind, defend the person from your criticisms as you would defend yourself from such unkindness. Then deliberately speak kindly about that person. Try it. You'll like it. This new habit of obedience will free you to be more lavish in the way you love others.

"Do not let any unwholesome talk come out of your mouths, but only what is helpful for building others up according to their needs, that it may benefit those who listen. And do not grieve the Holy Spirit of God, with whom you were sealed for the day of redemption. Get rid of all bitterness, rage and anger, brawling and slander, along with every form of malice. Be kind and compassionate to one another, forgiving each other, just as in Christ God forgave you" (EPHESIANS 4:29–32).

NOVEMBER 17
Child,

Everything that comes out of you started on the inside of you. As you worship and adore Me, then line your attitude up with

Mine. The operating system you'll run today's events through will determine how effectively you will live in love. Start by determining beforehand that everything that happens today will have the mind of Christ as the operating system you're running. What am I seeing? How am I responding?

"In your relationships with one another, have the same mindset as Christ Jesus" (Philippians 2:5).

NOVEMBER 18
Child,

Has someone hurt you? Were you taken by surprise at a betrayal? Might I have stopped the hurtful event, but didn't? So, are you feeling let down by Me as well? You can embrace all your feelings of hurt, even hurt toward Me. I'm not fragile. But, settle in your mind: I could have stopped it but didn't. Can your next reality check be that there is a good and redemptive purpose hidden away in the situation? You don't have to know what it is, just that there is. Can you accept that your role is not to whine, scold, or wallow but to forgive? And to love? It will take a full surrender of every thought and attitude to Me, but here I am. I will do a work of forgiveness through you for which there will be no other explanation except Me. Will you be completely in this with Me?

"Therefore, as God's chosen people, holy and dearly loved, clothe yourselves with compassion, kindness, humility, gentleness and patience. Bear with each other and forgive one another if any of you has a grievance against someone. Forgive as the Lord forgave you. And over all these virtues put on love, which binds them all together in perfect unity" (Colossians 3:12–14).

NOVEMBER 19
Child,

Whatever you do today, do it with all your might. Everything you've got, put it into tasks big and small, as if I am the one who has assigned those very tasks. Because I *am* the one who has assigned those very tasks. I will supply supernatural wisdom where needed. I will supply energy. I will supply patience. Everything you need today to accomplish what I've called you to, task by task, just ask Me. Every act of work you do is worship—surrendered life, heart focused on Me. Just do the work.

"Be strong and courageous, and do the work. Do not be afraid or discouraged, for the LORD God, my God, is with you. He will not fail you or forsake you until all the work for the service of the temple of the LORD is finished" (1 CHRONICLES 28:20).

NOVEMBER 20
Child,

This day's responsibilities and this day's challenges and this day's joys are all that I have ordained for you on this day. Whatever comes up, just do what's in front of you. Live out the day one action at a time. Just do the day.

"Give us today our daily bread" (MATTHEW 6:11).

NOVEMBER 21
Child,

Don't let shame shape you. Everything about you has been redeemed, and even while that redemption is being worked out into the details of your life and personality, you don't have to hide aspects of yourself away as if they lessen your value. Don't let that which I have redeemed and am in the process of healing and restoring be targets for Satan's condemnation and accusations. Don't let your personality and ways of relating to others be formed around wounds in your soul that you are trying to keep under wraps. Just be you—the you that I have redeemed. I'm telling My story through your story. Let Me tell it My way.

"Praise be to the Lord, the God of Israel, because he has come to his people and redeemed them" (LUKE 1:68).

NOVEMBER 22
Child,

Your wait will not last forever. It is a season. It is an interlude that I have scheduled for you. It comes just at the right time in your life. It is necessary to the outcome I am producing. I can't accomplish what I intend without this period that requires you to be still while I do what only I can do. Trust that when it seems to you that I'm doing nothing, I'm really moving everything into place and working tirelessly toward a result that is more than you've asked.

"Another illustration from God's creation might be the incubation period during which a bird's fertilized egg reaches maturity and hatches a baby bird. Once a bird lays her eggs, she sits on them to incubate them. To the uninformed observer, it would appear that nothing is happening. That observer would be amazed if he knew just how much was happening. The incubating bird has tucked her eggs underneath her stomach feathers close to a bare spot called her brood

patch. The brood patch is the warmest surface on the bird's body because of the network of blood vessels that lie close to the surface and produce heat. This heat is readily passed from the mother bird to her eggs. Her waiting is deliberate. The delay is essential to the outcome. All the work is invisible to the physical eye. As the mother sits on her eggs, the embryo is growing to a fully formed chick. When the chick is fully formed, it will hatch. When the time is fulfilled, the chicks will be revealed."

—Jennifer Kennedy Dean, *Heart's Cry*

NOVEMBER 23
Child,

Bring Me all your broken things—broken heart, broken relationship, broken dream, broken faith, broken past. I restore broken things. I take the very thing you thought ruined and wrecked. I take it in My hands, and I reshape it into something spectacular and beautiful. All your trash becomes My treasure. All your rubble becomes the unprocessed material for Me to use to form you into a most magnificent creation.

"But the pot he was shaping from the clay was marred in his hands; so the potter formed it into another pot, shaping it as seemed best to him" (Jeremiah 18:4).

NOVEMBER 24
Child,

Love is what changes your actions from empty religious traditions or rituals into vital, life-giving actions. I have not called you to rote attendance to doctrine or formularized observances. I have called you to heart-deep, passionate love for Me. The outer expressions of your worship may look the same, but love will change them. Don't go through the motions today. Let love for Me animate your expressions of worship, not habit or tradition. Let love rule you.

"Our god is the person we think is the most precious, for whom we would make the greatest sacrifice, who moves our hearts with the warmest love. He or it is the person who, if we lost him, would leave us desolate."

—ALAN REDPATH

NOVEMBER 25
Child,

Listen *to* Me, and listen *for* Me. Give Me time to speak. Expect My voice. I created words to be the way that one person's thoughts are communicated to another. I'm a wordy God. I talk all the time. My Son is the Word made flesh. I know how to speak words to you. Hear Me.

"We must be able to hear from God because He alone is the source of true prayer. His desires pour into our hearts so that they become our desires and are expressed through our words—this is the goal of the praying life."

—JENNIFER KENNEDY DEAN, *Live a Praying Life*

NOVEMBER 26
Child,

I don't always speak to you in sentences. Most of the time, I speak to you in the natural rhythms of your personality. I make direct deposits to your mind and your heart. It is not mystical or mysterious. It is the way I have created life to flow once you and I are joined together by My Spirit. Stay grounded in My Word, and let My Word be the infrastructure of your thought life. I will speak My words through My Word, and My living words will take up residence and live in you.

"As the rain and the snow come down from heaven, and do not return to it without watering the earth and making it bud and flourish, so that it yields seed for the sower and bread for the eater, so is my word that goes out from my mouth: It will not return to me empty, but will accomplish what I desire and achieve the purpose for which I sent it" (ISAIAH 55:10–11).

NOVEMBER 27
Child,

Where is there discord in your relationships? I know you can quickly see how the other person is responsible for any problems. But I'm calling you to an act of courage and confidence in Me. Let's look at your side of the equation. Don't come at this in a defensive posture. Be open and vulnerable. As I show you your errors, don't counter-argue with the other person's corresponding, or worse, actions. Just let Me show you where you can walk in more freedom by letting go of defensiveness and the need to assign blame elsewhere. I love you and only want you to know what it means to walk in My love. If you only love those who agree with you, or whose personality and outlook jell with yours, then you have not had to call on supernatural love. My love poured into your heart will love those whom you cannot. And, for the sake of love, you can let down your guard and fully embrace exactly the person who is so hard for you to love.

"I want the love that cannot help but love; loving, like God, for very sake of love."

—A. B. SIMPSON

NOVEMBER 28
Child,

You have been called into a priesthood. You have a very specific function and responsibility. You are to represent Me to others. Wherever I have intersected your life with others—family, church, work, neighborhood—My intention is that you would be My representative there. You are to be the conductor of My life there, like power flows through a conductive substance. That's why you are there. Not only do you have a function, you also have an empowering anointing in the person of My Spirit. I have called you, assigned you, and empowered you. Go.

"But you are a chosen people, a royal priesthood, a holy nation, God's special possession, that you may declare the praises of him who called you out of darkness into his wonderful light" (1 Peter 2:9).

NOVEMBER 29
Child,

I will work in your life in such a way that you will have firsthand experience of Me. Then you will know that what you have heard and believed is absolutely dependable. This is how I settle faith and give it roots. I do what I say. What My mouth promises, My hand performs.

"I am watching to see that my word is fulfilled" (Jeremiah 1:12).

NOVEMBER 30

Child,

Don't have anxiety about anything, anything at all. This is not a command I'm expecting you to follow by just choosing not to be anxious. You are not able to accomplish that. This is a promise I'm making you. You don't have to embrace and nurture anxiety because you are Mine. Accept My peace. Let My supernatural peace that has nothing to do with circumstances flow right from Me into you.

"I have told you these things, so that in me you may have peace. In this world you will have trouble. But take heart! I have overcome the world" (JOHN 16:33).

December

DECEMBER 1
Child,

Your faith is not measured in emotion, but in action. You may feel as if you have no faith, or not enough faith. But you will find when you obey Me, that you do indeed have faith, and the feelings of faith will find you. It's all about obedience.

"The Bible recognizes no faith that does not lead to obedience, nor does it recognize any obedience that does not spring from faith. The two are at opposite sides of the same coin."

—A. W. TOZER

DECEMBER 2
Child,

Watch today for how you can serve, not how you can be served. When the Word became flesh, My Son left the highest place and voluntarily took the lowest place. He has forever exalted the humblest acts of service, done in obscurity and anonymity. Your action of service to the least of these is how you bow low before Me. I receive it as precious worship and it is a sweet-smelling aroma to Me.

"Whoever wants to become great among you must be your servant, and whoever wants to be first must be your slave—just as the Son of Man did not come to be served, but to serve, and to give his life as a ransom for many" (MATTHEW 20:26–28).

DECEMBER 3
Child,

When I seem to be delaying, I am strategizing. I am timing everything just exactly. I am never procrastinating or withholding.

Right now, as you wait, strip away the lies that are twining in to your thinking—lies that tell you that I won't come through for you because you don't deserve it. Or that I'm waiting for you to pray a certain way that fits My formula, or that I don't desire good for you, only hardship and disappointment. Lies, all. Remember how My people longed to see the coming of Messiah while one generation after another waited and hoped. But the timing was always preplanned, and when all the pieces were in place, the Promised One appeared—at just the right time, in just the right way.

"But when the fullness of the time came, God sent forth His Son, born of a woman, born under the Law" (GALATIANS 4:4 NASB).

DECEMBER 4
Child,

Don't frontload your prayers with your expectations of what I should do. I have not pledged Myself to your best idea. I have pledged Myself to more than you could ask or imagine. When you try to decide for Me how to handle a situation, you will have your focus on the very narrowly drawn window of your anticipated answer, and you will miss what I'm doing. Those who were watching for the grand entrance of a mighty king as Messiah, missed the quiet birth in a stable.

"On earth, it was a little-noticed event. A young peasant couple and a few poor shepherds were the only witnesses to an ordinary birth in an ordinary place at an ordinary time. No pomp or ceremony. No grand announcement to a waiting crowd. No dancing in the streets. In the heavens, that which looked ordinary from the earth was the spark for unparalleled celebration (Hebrews 1:6). It was something never before seen and never to be seen again—when the King became a servant."

—JENNIFER KENNEDY DEAN, *Pursuing the Christ*

DECEMBER 5
Child,

I am right there in the middle of the ordinary. If you're waiting for a moment full of flourishes and grandstanding, you'll miss Me as I interrupt the ordinariness of your days with My grand presence. The setting into which I will come in all My glory is wherever you are, whatever you're doing. I astonished a teen-aged peasant girl named Mary in the middle of an unexceptional day full of banal tasks. Her response to My unexpected visit on that mundane day changed the course of history.

"Just as in prayer it is not we who momentarily catch His attention but He ours, so when we fail to hear His voice it is not because He is not speaking so much as that we are not listening. . . . We must recognize that all things are in God and that God is in all things, and we must learn to be very attentive, in order to hear God speaking in His ordinary tone without any special accent."
—Charles H. Brent, *With God in the World: A Series of Papers*

DECEMBER 6
Jesus,

Our salvation was of such importance to You that You emptied Yourself (Philippians 2:7). You who were full of all the fullness of God, emptied Yourself to become a servant. You who were everything, made Yourself nothing. Receiving You as my Savior requires that I humble myself and empty myself of myself and welcome You as my Everything. When I contrast the act of humility required of me to receive Your gift and the act of humility required of You to give such a great salvation, I am left speechless with wonder.

"Christ is the humility of God embodied in human nature; the Eternal Love humbling itself, clothing itself in the garb of meekness and gentleness, to win and serve and save us."

—Andrew Murray, *Humility and Absolute Surrender*

DECEMBER 7

Father,

You make such use of my weakness. You enter my life at the points of my weakness and make my weakness Your megaphone. As You work in me that which I cannot accomplish, and do through me that which I cannot achieve, You announce Yourself to the people in my world. You don't need my strength. You bring the strength. I surrender all my weakness to Your strength.

"Only You could have devised and then implemented such a plan. Only You could have found the way for heaven to invade earth, not through force or might, but through a tiny newborn baby. Your entry points in my life are not the things about me that are strong. Those things have the potential to keep my life closed to Your appearing. Your entry points into my life are those places where I am weak. Fill my weaknesses with Your power."

—Jennifer Kennedy Dean, *Pursuing the Christ*

DECEMBER 8

Child,

You only see a small piece of the story. You can't see what lies ahead. You can't see what I can see. Don't respond to the present moment. Instead, wait for the story to unfold. When a young carpenter in Nazareth heard that his intended wife was pregnant, what conclusions could he possibly have drawn? He based his first assumption on the obvious facts. When he followed the facts, they lead to only one assumption. But the facts as he knew them were not the whole story. What he saw first as disaster and the end of a dream, was, in fact, triumph and the beginning of redemption. What you see today is not telling the whole story. Wait patiently for Me.

"I wait for the L*ORD, my whole being waits, and in his word I put my hope. I wait for the Lord more than watchmen wait for the morning, more than watchmen wait for the morning"* (P*SALM* 130:5–6).

DECEMBER 9
Child,

My love plans ahead. I see your failings, and your hurts, and your struggles before you know anything about them, and I plan ahead. Before I created the earth, I saw the sin that would poison My beloved humanity, and I planned ahead. On a night in Bethlehem when a baby was born in a stable and laid in a manger, you can see My way of dealing with My people. Before the need arises, the answer is in place. When My Son took on flesh, it was the consummation of a promise made in the garden when sin first entered. Before a sin was ever committed, a plan was in motion for redemption. Be assured, in your life, I have planned ahead.

"Before they call I will answer; while they are still speaking I will hear" (I*SAIAH* 65:24).

DECEMBER 10
Child,

When My Son was born on earth, My long-planned blueprint for salvation was revealed in a tiny squirmy newborn. Until Him, earth was devoid of the kind of peace that fills heaven. Heaven's peace couldn't get to earth's inhabitants. But My Son brought it with Him. His life was the portal through which heaven could reach Earth. Now you have the offer of His peace. Not the world's peace, but heaven's peace. Don't depend on the unstable kind of pseudo-peace you might find for fleeting moments in the world. Don't settle for come-and-go peace. Here, take My peace.

"Peace I leave with you; my peace I give you. I do not give to you as the world gives. Do not let your hearts be troubled and do not be afraid" (JOHN 14:27).

DECEMBER 11
Child,

Today, live in an attitude of receptivity to Me. Receive everything as from My hand, because it is so. Every good gift is from Me. Every challenge or disappointment is with My permission and has all the destruction strained out of it through the sieve of My love. So, thank Me all day long—for everything. This is a season of giving and receiving. Let it be a season when you remember to live with open hand toward Me. That's not rude. It delights Me for you to be always looking to Me for provision.

"Faith is two empty hands held open to receive all of the Lord."
—ALAN REDPATH

DECEMBER 12
Father,

Thank You for providing a salvation that assures my rescue from any of Satan's tactics or schemes. Though I have an enemy intent on my destruction, I have a God and Savior who has already ensured his defeat and my victory. Today, I keep my thoughts focused on the triumph that is mine and refuse to be distracted by the bullying tactics of my preemptively defeated foe.

"Your battle gear looked to those on earth like the soft skin of a newborn baby. But nothing could have been more devastating to the enemy seeking my defeat. You invaded his territory. You staged a surprise rescue operation. You assaulted his base camp and released his prisoners of war. Prince of Peace, this peace You have offered me was won with the shedding of Your blood. You, who could have stayed above the fray, instead entered in full force."

—Jennifer Kennedy Dean, *Pursuing the Christ*

DECEMBER 13
Child,

When the little, tiny body of newborn Jesus transported heaven's riches into earth's atmosphere, the great expanse of heaven's riches were compacted. Like garments packed into a small suitcase, they had to be unfolded and shaken out. You see how, as Jesus grew from infancy into manhood, more and more of heaven's power and provision were put on display in Him— infant, little boy, teenager, man, Savior. At the Cross, everything was unpacked: all the purpose of His incarnation flying high out in the open like a flag. It's all out now. All the power and provision heaven has is yours in Jesus. Take it. Use it. Accept it.

"We believe that to Christ belongs creative power—that 'without Him was not anything made which was made.' We believe that from Him came all life at first. In Him life was as in its deep source. He is the fountain of life. We believe that as no being comes into existence without His creative power, so none continues to exist without His sustaining energy. We believe that the history of the world is but the history of His influence, and that the centre of the whole universe is the cross of Cavalry."

—Alexander Maclaren

DECEMBER 14
Jesus,

Why would the Beloved become the Despised? Why would heaven's Darling become the lightning rod for heaven's wrath? What was in it for You, Jesus? You didn't gain more glory. You didn't gain more power, or more adoration. But I think You gained more joy. "For the joy set before [You], [You] endured the cross, scorning its shame" (Hebrews 12:2). So what brought You such joy? What did You have because of the Crucifixion that You didn't have before the Crucifixion? All I can see that You gained—that accounted for the joy set before You—is that You gained us. Are we—am I—that precious to You that Your joy was not full until You had won our salvation? The imponderable mystery of "why," when I consider Your incarnation, leads me to this breathtaking conclusion: we complete Your joy. We are the prize You won.

"We have a saying that is meant to demean the value of someone. 'She's no prize,' we might say sarcastically. Isn't it amazing to know that Jesus thinks just the opposite? 'What a prize you are!' He says to you. 'Worth everything you cost Me!' When Jesus chose to run the race marked out for Him, He did it to obtain a promise. He wasn't running just to run. He was running to win the prize."

—Jennifer Kennedy Dean, *Life Unhindered*

DECEMBER 15
Father,

Until You had secured our salvation, was heaven not enough? Was there such a longing for Your people that even the joys and glory of heaven could not fill Your heart? When I ponder Your ravishing love for us, how ashamed I am that I ever, ever grow cold or distant toward You. That I could ever allow anything to distract Me from Your presence. Could I really—even for a second—forget to remember what I am to You? It calls out a love for You that is indescribable. I love You because You first loved me.

"This is love: not that we loved God, but that he loved us and sent his Son as an atoning sacrifice for our sins" (1 John 4:10).

DECEMBER 16
Child,

Learn that I come in unexpected ways. I don't have a box to be outside of, so *outside the box* doesn't really say it. You can't predict Me. You can't define boundaries within which I will do My work. I'm quirky. Eccentric even. Look at the way I opened the salvation story. God of all creation, reduced to a cluster of cells clinging to the lining of a virgin's womb. Born in blood and pain and bodily fluids, and bedded in an animal's trough. While everyone else was looking one direction, I slipped the Savior quietly into the world from a completely unexpected direction. You have to keep Your eyes on Me, or you'll miss what I'm doing.

"When we lose one blessing, another is often most unexpectedly given in its place."
—C. S. Lewis

DECEMBER 17
Jesus,

You dwell in unapproachable light. Unapproachable—can't come near to; off-putting; away-pushing. In Your natural habitat, we can't get to You. You're too glorious, too utterly other, too bright and shining. Maybe if we could veil our faces—maybe then we could at least view You from a safe distance. But get right into Your presence? Unapproachable light rules out that possibility. Except that You changed the dynamics of the situation. So that we would not have to veil our faces, You veiled Your glory. You dressed in flesh and blood and stepped down into our tawdry, lackluster world and became the Light in our darkness. Oh, glory!

"The Word became flesh and made his dwelling among us. We have seen his glory, the glory of the one and only Son, who came from the Father, full of grace and truth" (JOHN 1:14).

DECEMBER 18
Jesus,

My heart is captivated today by the lengths to which You are willing to go to love me. Me! As I think about You as the Word made flesh who was God from the beginning, who could have stayed safely ensconced in heaven, but chose to come *down* to me. Down! The opposite of where we think God should be headed. You took on our DNA and our limitations and our vulnerabilities so You could be God With Us. Not calling out from Your rarified perch, "Come here to Me!" but rather stepping down into our messiness, coming *to us*. Calling each of us by name. In Your pursuit of us, no holds barred. All in.

"But he was pierced for our transgressions, he was crushed for our iniquities; the punishment that brought us peace was on him, and by his wounds we are healed" (ISAIAH 53:5).

DECEMBER 19

Father,

I'm wondering—what must it have been like for Joseph when he first heard the horrifying news about his betrothed, and then listened to her ridiculous explanation? Did he wonder if she was trying to make him look like a fool? Did his pride get all wrapped around the situation? Then, You called on him to stand by Mary and carry out his role in her life, even though everyone knew the humiliating facts. He probably rightly assumed that questions about the parentage of the child would follow him, and that there would be gossiping and speculating behind his back for the rest of his life. He, a righteous and devout man, through no fault of his own became a laughingstock. But he chose to obey You and consider Your pleasure in his obedience of more value than any person's opinion. Father, I want my heart to be as completely Yours as was Joseph's. Teach me to live for an audience of One.

"The only humility that is really ours is not that which we try to show before God in prayer, but that which we carry with us, and carry out in our ordinary conduct."

—ANDREW MURRAY, *Humility*

DECEMBER 20

Child,

Look at the shepherds and notice the impulsive response to meeting Jesus. They could not contain the news, and they could not constrain their wonder. They told anyone who would listen, and they praised Me and glorified Me. Just a glimpse of Jesus and worship flows freely from the lips and from the life. No one who has seen Jesus face-to-face has to have a sermon or a seminar to teach them to respond in worship. Let your mind's eye come to rest on Jesus today, and then do what comes naturally.

"When they had seen him, they spread the word concerning what had been told them about this child, and all who heard it were amazed at what the shepherds said to them. . . . The shepherds returned, glorifying and praising God for all the things they had heard and seen, which were just as they had been told" (LUKE 2:17–20).

DECEMBER 21
Child,

I will break into your life at odd junctures and in unexpected ways. Always make room for Me to interrupt you. Like shepherds keeping watch over their flocks, you may be engaged in the accustomed cadences of your life when the ground shifts beneath you and My glory shines round about you, heaven sings you a new song. Be ready. Be where you're supposed to be doing what you're supposed to be doing, and all the while, be ready.

"And there were shepherds living out in the fields nearby, keeping watch over their flocks at night. An angel of the Lord appeared to them, and the glory of the Lord shone around them, and they were terrified. . . . Suddenly a great company of the heavenly host appeared with the angel, praising God" (LUKE 2:8–13).

DECEMBER 22
Jesus,

To secure my salvation, You came to earth as a man. You did not just dress up like a man, or disguise yourself as a man, or pretend to be a man. You became a man. You left behind Your inherent power as God, though not Your nature as God, to live in the form of a man, obedient to the Father and empowered and led by the Spirit. You took on our vulnerabilities and needs and lived out Your life on earth in complete dependence on and faith in the Father. You could afford to lay aside your power as God because You knew it was perfectly safe to live by fully trusting the Father. So, being so fully man that You arrived on earth as a newborn baby completely exposed to all of earth's dangers, was no stretch for You.

"Very truly I tell you, the Son can do nothing by himself; he can do only what he sees his Father doing, because whatever the Father does the Son also does" (JOHN 5:19).

DECEMBER 23
Child,

Pain has an end. Let Me comfort you today. Let Me speak tenderly to you. Cast your eyes forward in hope. I have made plans for you, to give you a future and a hope. From the beginning, sin's goal was to snuff out all hope, but I took that power from the enemy's hands. As soon as sin disrupted My perfect creation, I put hope into the picture. I announced My redemption plan from the beginning, and began immediately to lay the groundwork that would lead to that first Christmas when My long-ago promise was set in motion at just the right time, in just the right way. I am laying groundwork for the plan I have for your life, and it will be as I have promised. The blessings will be double the pain.

"Comfort, comfort my people, says your God. Speak tenderly to Jerusalem, and proclaim to her that her hard service has been completed, that her sin has been paid for, that she has received from the LORD's hand double for all her sins" (ISAIAH 40:1–2).

DECEMBER 24
Child,

I am never bound by convention. I rarely act as expected. When the dictates of a religious tradition grow inflexible like old wineskins, My life is not in residence there. I am always flowing and active and carving out new paths. My ways are not predictable. You can count on Me to keep My promises, but you are very unlikely to predict My ways. My ways are past finding out. How I will do what I do will surprise and thrill you. Save the world by sending My Son in the form of a baby—not predictable. You think I'm not working because when you look at all the expected ways, you don't see Me. What I'm doing on your behalf right now will not fit into old wineskins. My promise to you will slip into your life from a new and unanticipated direction.

"Did you never run to a tree for shelter in a storm, and find fruit which you expected not? Did you never go to God for safeguard in these times, driven by outward storms, and there find unexpected fruit . . .?"

—John Owen

DECEMBER 25
Child,

Today, celebrate Me. Be reminded that My love for you is such that I would bend low to seek you out and pursue you. I would leave the comforts and glories of heaven just so I could bring you home with Me (John 17:24). Whatever emotions might assail you on this day of celebration, stay grounded in My love for you. This is a vulnerable day. Let your vulnerabilities be sheltered by My love.

"'Surely God is my salvation; I will trust and not be afraid. The Lord, *the* Lord *himself, is my strength and my defense; he has become my salvation;' With joy you will draw water from the wells of salvation"* (Isaiah 12:2–3).

DECEMBER 26
Child,

Let Me into every part of your life. The things you are trying to manage and fix in your own power are instead getting a tighter strangle hold on you. Like a spider's web, the more you struggle to be free, the tighter the grip it gains. You feel like a failure. Hope is slowly disappearing. You are on the verge of deciding that change in this area is an unrealistic expectation. Let Me in.

"It is not a matter of our doing our best for Him, but of *Christ being His best in us.* All that He is in all that we are! We can never have more . . . and need never enjoy less. Just receive and say, 'Thank You!'"

—Major W. Ian Thomas, *The Indwelling Life of Christ*

DECEMBER 27
Child,

Everything I do in your life has one purpose: to conform you into the image of My Son. I conform you by His life in you transforming you from the inside, and flowing through you on the outside. The more you are shaped from within by His presence, the more natural it is for Him to work through you in your world. You must decrease and He must increase.

"Paul is saying, 'I am a redeemed sinner, and the risen Jesus has come to reinvade my humanity so that He can serve with my hands, walk with my feet, speak with my lips, see with my eyes, hear with my ears, think with my mind, and love with my heart, so that to me, to live now is Christ. It is my privilege as a forgiven sinner to place my humanity at His disposal so that others looking at me will

see Him behaving, just as those who looked at Jesus saw His Father behaving.'"

—Major W. Ian Thomas, *The Indwelling Life of Christ*

DECEMBER 28
Child,

Faith grows by use. It's an investment you make. Invest all your faith in the situation you are facing right now. When the whole situation plays out all the way to the end, your faith will have increased. Stop trying to grow faith by effort or emotion. Stop trying to "have enough faith" before you invest it. Invest what you have, and let it grow.

"Again, it will be like a man going on a journey, who called his servants and entrusted his wealth to them. To one he gave five bags of gold, to another two bags, and to another one bag, each according to his ability. Then he went on his journey. The man who had received five bags of gold went at once and put his money to work and gained five bags more. So also, the one with two bags of gold gained two more. But the man who had received one bag went off, dug a hole in the ground and hid his master's money" (Matthew 25:14–18).

DECEMBER 29
Child,

In calling you to rest in Me, I am not calling you to be passive or inactive. I am calling you to let My energy work mightily in you. You will wear out and burn out, but I will not. When you gave yourself to Me, I gave Myself to you. Practice this prayer all day long, "Jesus, You do it." See what happens.

"Come to me, all you who are weary and burdened, and I will give you rest" (Matthew 11:28).

DECEMBER 30
Child,

I don't waste time. I don't run out the clock. Every minute of your life is divinely orchestrated so that it works out every detail of My purpose. Cooperate with now. See where it's taking you.

"You cooperate with the immediate inevitable because you know that in and through things God's will is being worked out."
—E. Stanley Jones (1884–1973), *American missionary*

DECEMBER 31
Child,

I don't call you *from* something without calling you *to* something. I don't call you to sacrifice for the sake of sacrifice, but for the sake of something more. I only ask you to let go of something so you can grab hold of something more precious. When you feel that I am taking something from you, it is only so I can give something to you. My love compels Me to give. No matter what things look like to you at any given moment, I am giving, not taking.

"The Lord had said to Abram, 'Go from your country, your people and your father's household to the land I will show you. I will make you into a great nation, and I will bless you; I will make your name great, and you will be a blessing. I will bless those who bless you, and whoever curses you I will curse; and all peoples on earth will be blessed through you.' So Abram went, as the Lord had told him" (Genesis 12:1–4).

New Hope® Publishers is a division of WMU®, an international organization
that challenges Christian believers to understand and be radically involved in
God's mission. For more information about WMU,
go to wmu.com. More information about New Hope books may be
found at NewHopeDigital.com. New Hope books may be
purchased at your local bookstore.

Use the QR reader on your
smartphone to visit us online at
NewHopeDigital.com

If you've been blessed by this book, we would like to hear your story.
The publisher and author welcome your comments and
suggestions at: newhopereader@wmu.org.

Bible Study On the Go!

Interact. Engage. Grow.

New Hope Interactive is a new digital Bible study platform that allows you to unlock content to download your favorite New Hope Bible study workbooks on your tablet or mobile device. Your answers and notes are kept private through a profile that's easy to create and FREE!

Perfect for individual or small group use!

To learn more visit NewHopeInteractive.com/getstarted

Other Dynamic Studies by This Author

Life Unhindered!
Five Keys to Walking in Freedom

ISBN-13: 978-1-59669-286-2
N104143 • $14.99

Live a Praying Life!
Open Your Life to God's Power and Provision

ISBN-13: 978-1-59669-299-2
N104149 • $19.99

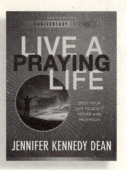

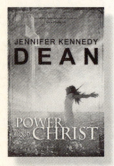

Power in the Blood of Christ

ISBN-13: 978-1-59669-363-0
N134106 • $14.99

Set Apart
A 6-Week Study of the Beatitudes

ISBN-13: 978-1-59669-263-3
N104132 • $14.99

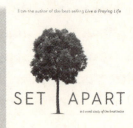

Available in bookstores everywhere. For information about these books or this author, visit NewHopeDigital.com.

NEW HOPE
PUBLISHERS
Gospel-Centered. Missions-Driven.